basic VST EFFECTS

Printed in the United Kingdom by MPG Books Ltd, Bodmin, Cornwall

Published by: Sanctuary Publishing Limited, Sanctuary House, 45-53 Sinclair Road, London W14 0NS, United Kingdom.
www.sanctuarypublishing.com

Sound On Sound website: www.sospubs.co.uk

ISBN: 1-86074-359-5

PAUL WHITE

Also by Paul White from Sanctuary Publishing

Audigy – The User Guide
Desktop Digital Studio
Creative Recording I – Effects & Processors
Creative Recording II – Microphones, Acoustics, Soundproofing & Monitoring
Home Recording Made Easy (Second Edition)
MIDI For The Technophobe
Live Sound For The Performing Musician
Recording & Production Techniques
Music Technology – A Survivor's Guide

Also in this series

basic DIGITAL RECORDING
basic EFFECTS AND PROCESSORS
basic HOME STUDIO DESIGN
basic LIVE SOUND
basic MASTERING
basic MICROPHONES
basic MIDI
basic MIXERS
basic MIXING TECHNIQUES
basic MULTITRACKING
basic VST INSTRUMENTS

contents

chapter 4

introduction

Until recently, studio effects and signal processors came as separate hardware boxes, but today you can also use software plug-ins that work within MIDI/audio sequencers and audio programs, all drawing their power from the host computer. The turning point for the user was Steinberg's Virtual Studio Technology initiative, or VST as it is more commonly known. Part of the VST concept is that additional functionality can be added to the host software by means of plug-in enhancements.

VST plug-ins are currently very popular because, when Steinberg opened up the VST system to third-party companies, they were embraced by many of the major players in the audio software world. Also, because the VST format relies entirely on the host computer's processor and memory for its operation, no additional hardware is needed to use the plug-ins. However, it follows that the more plug-ins you want to run at the same time, the more powerful a processor you'll need, as each takes up its share of the resources available.

Some plug-ins require more processing power than others, and a good reverb package can use up a significant proportion of your overall processing resources. Sophisticated denoising and declicking software is also processor intensive, while plug-ins such as delay and compression are less power hungry.

Plug-in effects and processors require no wiring, they don't take up space in your studio and you don't need a patchbay to connect them. Also, all of your plug-in effects settings can be saved along with your song data, you can automate parameters via MIDI and, once you've bought a plug-in, you can generally use several instances of it in the same song, with the practical limit on the amount of times that a plug-in may be used simultaneously being the amount of CPU power and RAM available.

Virtually any effect or processor that can exist in hardware form can be implemented in software, including compressors, equalisers, gates, reverb units, delay units, denoisers, declickers, vinyl emulators, pitch correctors and many more. There are even plug-ins that emulate vintage tube equipment and guitar amplifiers. The purpose of this book is to explore the VST environment and to look at the workings and applications of the different types of effects and processors available, concluding with some advice on using VST plug-ins to create a professional-sounding mix.

chapter 1

introduction to VST

In the traditional hardware recording studio, effects such as reverb and echo are generally handled by separate hardware units, but today many of those same effects are also available in software form for use within MIDI-plus-audio sequencers. Software-based effects and instruments have been around for many years, but until powerful desktop computers became available at an affordable price they were more of an academic curiosity than a practical tool for the majority of computer musicians. Furthermore, it was often difficult or impossible to integrate the computer effects that were available at that time into a sequencer package, as most were originally designed as stand-alone programs.

The first glimpse that most people got of software effects that could be accessed from within the host software was the Pro Tools system from Digidesign. This was developed at a time when computers were relatively low powered, so Digidesign used additional DSP cards to host specially written effect algorithms called *plug-ins* that could be called up from inside the Pro Tools software and slotted into its signal-routing architecture. As you might expect, such high-end technology came at a price, but once the potential of plug-ins had been realised, it was inevitable that somebody would find a way to make them work in more affordable systems. That somebody was the German music software manufacturing company Steinberg, who developed its VST (Virtual Studio Technology) system to work alongside Cubase MIDI-plus audio sequencer. The result was Cubase VST, which in its PC incarnation was also able to run Direct X plug-ins.

Following Digidesign's example, Steinberg opened up its VST protocol to third-party developers so that different software companies could create new effect plug-ins that could be used within Cubase. However, they then went one step further and allowed designers of other sequencers and audio programs to make use of the VST protocol as well. This single move was of huge benefit to computer music makers and software developers alike. Developers now only had to develop one version of their plug-ins to use in any VST program, while end users benefited from having a greater choice and lower prices, because of the economies of scale and competition.

Not every audio software company supports the VST protocol directly, however, although Steinberg (Cubase, Cubasis and WaveLab), Emagic (Logic Audio) and TC Works (Spark and Spark XL) do, and their audio software is by far the most popular in Europe. The USA-based Opcode system also supports VST, as does the Bias Peak stereo editor and the E-mu/Ensoniq Paris system. Mark Of The Unicorn's Digital Performer – which is particularly popular in the USA – has its own plug-in format, called MAS, but there are other programs that can effectively "wrap" a VST plug-in to make it work in a different plug-in environment. One such program is TC Works' Spark audio editor program, which includes a sophisticated effects-routing system within which one or more effects in various combinations can be wrapped and then used in any other VST- or MAS-compatible program. Similarly, Cakewalk Pro Audio 9 and Sonar can make use of VST plug-ins via the use of adaptor software.

The vast majority of music software runs on either Macintosh or PC computers, and there are often versions of the same software available for both platforms. Different versions of VST plug-ins are available, depending on whether the host software runs on a Mac or a PC, but most of the mainstream plug-ins are supplied with both versions on the same installation disk. However, be aware that there are some Mac plug-ins that aren't available for PCs and vice versa.

The original VST format evolved into VST II, a system in which the plug-ins are able to read MIDI information from the host sequencer. This opens up the possibility of automating plug-ins via MIDI, in much the same way as the mixer section of a sequencer can be automated, and it allows the user to link effects to the tempo of the sequencer. It also paved the way for the development of VST instruments, such as synthesisers and samplers, which are the subject of another book in this series called *basic VST INSTRUMENTS*.

VST plug-ins are said to be *native*, because they rely entirely on the host computer's processor and memory for their operation. From this, it follows that the more plug-ins you want to run at the same time, the more of your computer's processing power will be required. Even a modern powerful computer can do only a finite amount of work, so there will always be a limit to the number of VST effects that you can run at the same time as your sequencer or some other audio program. However, if you deploy your plug-ins with care, you shouldn't find this too limiting. Some plug-ins require more processing power than others, and a good reverb package can use up a significant proportion of your overall processing resources, while denoising and declicking software is also processor intensive, as are many virtual instruments.

VST plug-ins are used in different ways (depending on the host software package) that mirror the ways in which hardware effects are connected to conventional hardware mixers, via insert points and aux sends/returns. Stereo-editing packages, meanwhile, may use a simpler system where one or more plug-ins can be inserted in line with the audio signal path.

advantages of VST

VST plug-ins offer several advantages over their hardware counterparts. Most computer systems are based around soundcards or audio interfaces that have fewer inputs and outputs than a conventional mixer, so it may be physically impossible to connect a hardware effects unit in any way other than passing the entire output from a stereo soundcard through it. This is clearly very limiting, as the whole ethos of multitrack recording is based around the ability to process individual audio tracks in different ways. However, because VST plug-ins work within the host application, they can be patched into a sequencer's virtual mixer with the same flexibility as a hardware mixer.

VST plug-in effects and processors need no wiring, so there's no need for patchbays or cable, and they don't take up much space in your studio. Furthermore, you can save all of your plug-in settings along with your song data so that, when you return to a project after a long break, you don't have to try to remember which effects you used or how much of one effect was added to each channel.

With hardware effects, you pay for one box and you get one box, but with VST plug-ins you pay for one and you can use it as many times at once as your computer can support. For example, you can load in a compressor plug-in and then use that compressor six times in different channels of your virtual mixer, with different settings each time. The only limit on how many instances a plug-in may be used at the same time is the amount of DSP (Digital Signal Processing) power and RAM available.

types of VST plug-in

As I said, virtually any effect or processor that can exist in hardware form can be implemented in software. Even classic analogue equipment that uses tube circuitry can be emulated by modern modelling techniques, and there are software equivalents of famous-name compressors, equalisers, gates, reverbs and other devices currently on the market, as well as a huge range of plug-ins that have no direct hardware counterpart. VST plug-ins can also handle denoising, declicking and other audio-restoration jobs, and there are even plug-ins available for guitar players. Physical-modelling guitar amp simulators are popular for recording, but even these are available as VST plug-ins. Figure 1.1 shows a plug-in that faithfully models a TLA hardware equaliser.

More creative effects are also available, such as vocoders and ring modulators, and of course the dance music revolution has created a demand for plug-ins that add noise and crackle to a signal in order to simulate vinyl recordings and make the samples used in new recordings sound like they're taken from vinyl records. Also available are distortion devices, synth-style filters, rotary speaker

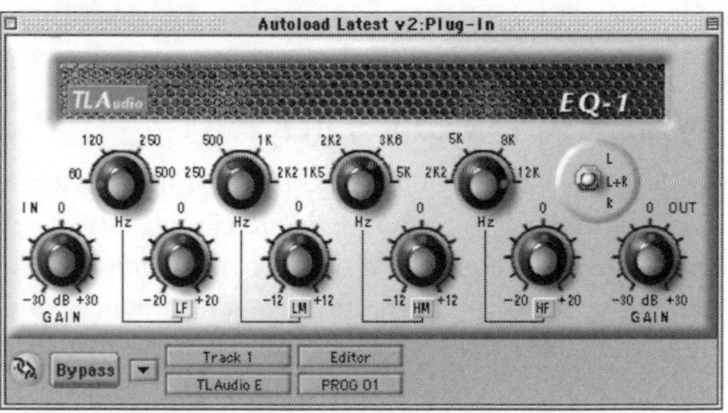

Figure 1.1: TLA equaliser plug-in

cabinet simulators and counterparts to just about every guitar pedal ever conceived.

One particularly exciting aspect of VST plug-ins is that software designers can create experimental effects and sophisticated processors that it would never have been possible to develop in hardware form at anything like the price. For instance, there are multiband fuzz boxes, pitch correctors designed to tune up imperfect vocal tracks, stereo-width enhancers, 3D sound-positioning algorithms, spectral enhancers and countless other gadgets available, all with the clear benefit of being operated via a sensibly sized virtual control panel instead of the small LCD window and cursor buttons familiar to any user of conventional hardware units. Indeed, computers can provide any kind of graphical interface, and so, as well as controls and meters, plug-ins often provide dynamic graphs showing compressor slopes, EQ curves and so on. Therefore, because of the importance of the visual user interface, and because sequencers tend to be based around several main windows that may need to be open simultaneously, it's advisable to buy a large monitor for your computer or even to configure the computer to run on two monitors. Figure 1.2 shows the Waves Q10 multiband equaliser, which has a very clear EQ curve display, on which it's possible to drag points on the EQ curve directly.

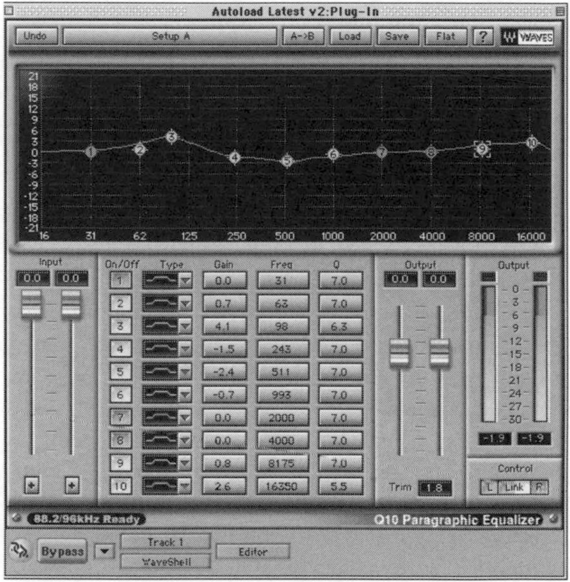

Figure 1.2: Waves' Q10 multiband equaliser

software protection

Nobody likes software that uses an anti-piracy system, as this can make it inconvenient for the legitimate user, but such measures are necessary to protect the intellectual property of the designers. If unlawful software copying isn't held in check, there will be no incentive for companies to design new products for us to use, and then we'll all lose out. You should also be aware that a lot of so-called "cracked" software fails to work properly and may even corrupt legitimately installed software that uses key-disk protection. There's also a real danger of picking up computer viruses, especially if the software was downloaded from the Internet. Figure 1.3 shows a screen shot of a cracked version of the AnTares Auto-Tune plug-in. Note that the hacker has put his logo over that of the manufacturer. It's tempting to get something for nothing, but it's best not to fall prey to temptation, as you'll be compromising not only the stability of your system but also the supply of future music software.

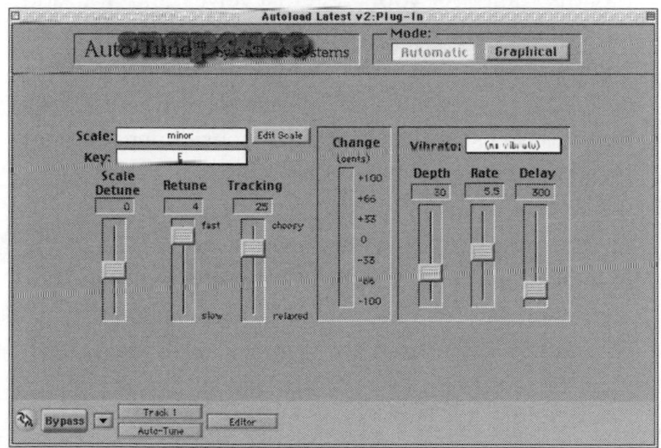

Figure 1.3: Pirated plug-in, displaying the hacker's logo

computing power

The ability to access virtual effects that can run in real time on a host computer is very attractive, but I must stress that you'll need the most powerful computer you can afford in order to make the most of them. Don't go by the minimum system requirements quoted by your software manufacturer, as this really is the bare minimum needed to make the host software run at all. As a rule of thumb, find out exactly how fast the fastest computer currently available is and then get one that's at least half or, ideally, three-quarters that speed. If you buy the very best, you'll probably pay over the odds and then get upset when the price tumbles in three months' time! As your system evolves and you add more plug-ins, you'll eventually need to upgrade your computer again, but given that a state-of-the-art PC can cost little more than just one good hardware effects box, this isn't such a bad trade-off, considering the extra plug-in power you'll have at your disposal.

Always make sure that you have more RAM than the minimum specified. Use the CPU usage meter in your audio software to determine the percentage of your computer's power that the plug-ins are using. RAM is very cheap now, so why not just add another 256MB?

Make sure that you don't push your computer to the

limit, or it will crash at the most inconvenient moment, and keep an eye on your software's CPU and disk drive usage meters. One useful tip is to zoom out of your sequencer's song window so that the whole song is visible. This prevents the peak in CPU drain that usually occurs whenever the screen is forced to scroll or redraw and can sometimes make the difference between your computer running smoothly and falling over during audio playback, when the CPU is heavily loaded.

VST plug-ins for editing

Stereo editors are somewhat different to sequencers, as they're designed to work with just two audio tracks, for editing up new arrangements and for assembling mixes in the correct running order for an album. For this, VST plug-in support is important, as mastering invariably involves some signal processing, most notably equalisation and compression. More serious mastering may involve the use of multiband compressors and precision peak limiters, and these are also available in VST plug-in form from certain manufacturers. Of course, as VST is standard, you can use any of your VST plug-ins in any of your VST-compatible audio programs – you're not restricted to using mastering plug-ins in only mastering programs. One very popular plug-in for use in mastering is the Waves L1 limiter, shown in Figure 1.4.

Figure 1.4: Waves' L1 Ultramaximizer plug-in

turbo VST?

Users have often asked, quite reasonably, if it's possible for somebody to develop some kind of accelerator card that will fit into a computer's PCI slot to enable the system to host more VST plug-ins. I've asked this same question of several manufacturers in the field, and their answer is that it wouldn't be practical at anything like a realistic price. The problem is that the CPU in your computer uses *floating-point mathematics*, while the high-speed DSP chips that could be used to build a cost-effective PCI accelerator work on *fixed-point arithmetic*. This difference means that the plug-in software would have to be completely rewritten to run on the DSP chips, in which case it would no longer be a standard VST plug-in. Nevertheless, at the time of writing, there are at least two companies that are currently building DSP cards designed to run specially written plug-ins that can be accessed from within a VST environment: TC Works' PowerCore and the Universal Audio Unity DSP card. Even though these aren't true VST plug-ins, once the card is installed they can be used as if they were within any VST-compatible program. Such cards can provide four or more times as much processing power as the host computer, which is good news if you want to run processor-intensive effects such as high-quality reverb.

Such cards can be designed to be run quite independent of the soundcard or audio interface that you're using, so there should be no compatibility issues. All that's required is that your host audio software is VST compatible. At the time of writing, PowerCore only supported the Macintosh platform, but PC support was anticipated to be included at around the end of 2001 or the beginning of 2002. The Unity card, meanwhile, wasn't available for testing, although it is scheduled to be available in both Mac and PC formats.

VST or not VST?

Some software comes complete with built-in effects that can be used in the same way as VST effects and freely mixed with true VST effects, but they're not actually VST plug-ins at all. For example, Emagic's Logic Audio range of programs comes complete with a generous suite of effects and processors, but these are actually integrated into the host program and so can't be used as VST plug-ins within other programs. In all other respects, however, they behave just like VST plug-ins and can be loaded into the same locations within Logic Audio's audio mixer. Figure 1.5 shows the Logic Audio Spectral Gate plug-in, which has the same styling as all of the other Logic effects.

Meanwhile, TC Works' Spark XL takes a similar approach with its DeNoise and DeClick modules, which

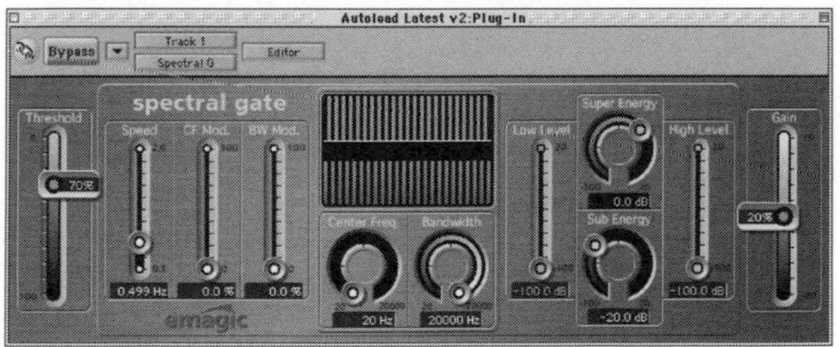

Figure 1.5: Logic Audio Spectral Gate

can be used in Spark's effects matrix in exactly the same way as regular VST plug-ins. However, Spark owners can use Spark's ability to "wrap" its FX Machine matrix – including the DeNoise and DeClicking functions – for use in other VST applications that are running on the machine for which Spark is authorised.

Some other manufacturers – including TC Works and Steinberg – are protecting the VST-plug-ins that they bundle with their host software in order to prevent them from being copied and used with different VST-compatible software on a different computer. In general, this scheme allows the plug-ins to be used with any VST-compatible program on the same computer as the one on which their host program is authorised to run, but the plug-in is no longer available if the host software is removed or de-authorised.

understanding effects

The term *VST effects* actually encompasses both effects and processors. Effects include things like reverb, chorus, echo and flanging, while processors include compressors, gates, pitch correctors and so on. It's important to draw a distinction between effects and processors, as there are limitations to how the two can be connected, and the next chapter examines this important area in detail. It's also important to know what all of the basic studio effects and processors do, and all of the standard effects and their key parameters will be explained in Chapter 3.

chapter 2

installing and using VST plug-ins

On the whole, VST plug-ins are easy to install, as both Mac and Windows versions come with largely automated installation routines. There are few exceptions, of course, and in these cases you'll need to follow the manufacturers' instructions carefully. The most important thing is to ensure that your plug-ins end up in the "VstPlugins" folder used by your audio software. If, after installation, your plug-in isn't available from within the plug-in menu, go back to the installation routine and make sure that all of the files are installed where they should be. It may be that you have two or more different VST folders on your hard drive and the plug-ins have been installed in the wrong one. For precise details, check the manual that came with your host software package and find out how VST plug-ins are accessed and whether you need to place the files in folders manually. If they're not in the right place, your software won't be able to find them and they won't show up in the VST Plug-ins menus.

In addition to the plug-ins themselves, there may also be libraries of presets (which are usually housed in the VST folder), and occasionally files are installed in the "System" folder. You may also be unable to locate a plug-in when you're looking for a mono plug-in when the insert point you're working on is in a stereo signal path. As a rule, in this case, only relevant plug-ins are visible.

I'm told that very few people bother to register their software purchases, but this is definitely a mistake. Once you register, you'll be notified of any updates or special deals and you'll also be entitled to a degree of product support. What's more, if you have a problem with authorisation, or if you change your computer, the fact that you've registered will confirm that you're the official owner of the software. If you haven't registered, you could just be somebody trying to bluff an authorisation for a pirate copy.

authorisation

If the software is copy protected, as most commercial music software is, you should see a message telling you what to do the first time you start up the software. Some software requires you to enter a serial number, and this is often found on the software packaging or on one of the pieces of paperwork inside the box. These are easy to lose, so I always take the precaution of writing the serial number on the label side of the installation disk with a felt-tipped pen. It might also be wise to create a Notepad file on the computer and keep copies of all of your serial numbers and challenge-and-response codes.

Those using dual-processor Macintosh G4 computers should note that not all VST plug-ins are able to work in Dual Processor mode, and these frequently cause the computer to lock up or crash. If you experience this problem, either switch off the computer's Dual Processor mode or temporarily remove any incompatible plug-ins from the "VstPlugins" folder before running the audio software that uses them.

copy protection

Most music software tends to be protected against unauthorised copying, which can be inconvenient for the legitimate user, but in the long term it should lead to better product support and lower prices. Protection comes in several forms, the most common for modern VST plug-ins being the uncopyable master CD-ROM and the challenge-and-response code. Some software is also authorised by means of a master key floppy disk, but as floppy drives are virtually obsolete, such systems are being phased out.

disk-based protection

Key-disk-install copy protection relies on an uncopyable master floppy disk, from which the software is installed. The master disk includes a counter that is decremented when the software is installed and incremented when the software is uninstalled. During installation, a hidden file is placed on the computer's hard drive, ensuring that the software will only work on that particular computer. When there are no more installations left, the only way to get the master disk to work again is to uninstall the software, again using the master disk.

If you need to change computers or reformat your hard drive, you'll first have to uninstall all of your copy-protected software. Note that users of Macintosh G4s or other Apple models that use external USB floppy drives may need a software patch to enable their drive to authorise their software. Most software of this kind is protected by a system developed by PACE, and the patch you'll need can be downloaded from www.paceap.com.

CD copy protection

The use of an uncopyable CD-ROM as the master disk is less intrusive than the master floppy disk system, and it's also less likely that to become damaged or corrupted. The software is installed from this CD-ROM in the normal way, but on random occasions (usually when that program is starting up) you'll be asked to insert the master CD-ROM before you can continue to work. More polite software gives you a period of grace during which you can continue working before inserting the CD-ROM after issuing a request that you do so. Then again, some software only needs to see the master CD-ROM once after you first install the software, although it may be required again if any major system changes are made.

challenge and response

If you've installed software that relies on "challenge-and-response" security, a set of words, numbers or characters is generated that is unique to your computer system. These will then need to be emailed or faxed to the software manufacturer, who will issue you with another set of codes to type into your computer that will authorise your software to run on that particular computer. You'll usually get a week or two to use the software prior to authorising it, although after this the program will time out unless you enter the correct response code. If you change computers, you'll need to notify the software manufacturer so that it can issue a new code.

deploying plug-ins

Just like hardware rack devices, VST effects have to be placed in the right part of the signal chain to make sense. There are numerous possible connection options, and the right one for you will depend on your host software package. The most flexible connection systems tend to be associated with software that includes an audio mixer. These programs allow effect and processor plug-ins to be connected in much the same way as they would be in a hardware mixer, and you'll find that all sequencers with multitrack audio capability include audio mixers. Stereo-editing programs, on the other hand, have no need of mixing facilities, although some offer very flexible effect/processor plug-in routing, such as TC Works' Spark program, which is covered later in this chapter.

the virtual mixer

The mixer sections of multitrack audio software tend to mirror many of the functions of hardware mixers. As I said, though, stereo editors don't require a mixer, so plug-ins are generally available as insert effects only. What is important in the context of VST effects and processors is knowing whereabouts in the signal path they can be used, and in this respect it's important to draw a distinction between effects and processors (even though both tend to be called "VST effects"). The reason for making this distinction is that there are some restrictions on how processors can be connected. Remember that in programs such as Logic Audio, which has a number of effects and processor plug-ins built into the program, these native plug-ins can be used in exactly the same way as true VST plug-ins and in combination with true VST plug-ins. However, they can't be used in other VST-compatible programs, because they're not true VST plug-ins.

The main distinction between effects and processors is that, with a processor, the entire signal passes through it, whereas with an effect it's more usual for some of the original (dry) signal to be added to some of the effected signal.

connection restrictions

While it is permissible to connect any type of effect or signal processor via an insert point, connections via the aux send/return system are strictly limited to effects only. (Both methods of connecting plug-ins will be described later in this chapter.) Even then, as a general rule, only delay-based effects such as reverb, echo, chorus, phasing, flanging and pitch shifting should be connected via the aux system. If the plug-in uses delay, and if there's a dry/effect mix knob or parameter, the plug-in is almost certain to be an effect.

A processor – such as EQ or a compressor – is unlikely to include delay as one of its elements and so should only be connected via insert points, not via aux sends. While there are some exceptions when using analogue mixers, as a means of working around certain mixer limitations, it's safest to stick to these rules when using virtual mixers.

Audio mixers are able to combine two or more audio signals and to allow their levels to be independently adjusted. This applies to both hardware and virtual mixers, and a typical virtual mixer will include equalisation (which is a type of processor) and have the ability to route signals and sub-mixes of signals to different destinations. Plug-ins work like software rack boxes, which can be patched into the mixer's signal path at certain strategic points, and there are two possible connection protocols: via aux sends and via insert points.

auxiliaries

The secret to using effects economically in any mixer is the aux control, as this allows an effect such as reverb or echo to be shared between any number of mixer channels. By using different settings of the post-fade aux control on each channel, it's possible to send different amounts of each channel's signal to the same effects unit. Effects are normally connected to a post-fade aux send; the pre-fade sends are there to provide an alternative cue (or monitor) mix for the performers, which may prove desirable if a singer needs to hear more of his vocals than of the instrumental backing.

Post-fade sends take their signal sources from after the channel fader (ie post-fader), and as a consequence the send level is affected by changes in the channel-fader setting. The unaffected (or dry) signal goes directly via the channel fader into the stereo mix buss, while the effect output is added to the main stereo mix (or to a group, if that's where you routed it). If you were to use a pre-fade send to feed an effect, the dry portion of the signal would change with the channel fader but the effect level would stay the same.

sends in Cubase VST

In Cubase VST, the aux sends are accessed by clicking the FX/EQ button in the audio mixer channel strips, where up to eight different aux sends per channel can be set up, if required, each feeding a different VST effect plug-in. The plug-ins are displayed in a pictorial representation of an effects rack, with the parameters shown in a virtual window. A virtual power button acts as a bypass function, and when an effect or processor is bypassed, no parameter values appear in the effects rack window. The effects assigned to the rack are chosen from a pull-down menu that is integral to the rack window, and the effect name will also be shown in the "button" relevant to the channel send control.

The available pages and parameters can be moved around with the cursor keys, while you can change the parameters via a data entry-type knob. Most of the more sophisticated plug-ins have an alternative "view" modelled on a virtual front panel equipped with multiple controls that can be adjusted in real time. (Note that simplified versions of Cubase, such as Cubasis, limit the number of aux sends that can be set up.) Figure 2.1 shows a Cubasis effects rack window.

sends in Logic Audio

Emagic's Logic Audio handles aux sends slightly differently. Again, the individual channels can access up to eight aux send knobs. However, rather than being routed directly to the effects plug-ins, these are routed to buss channels. The desired effects are then placed in insert points within the buss channels and the outputs

Figure 2.1: Aux sends in Cubasis

of the busses are routed back into the stereo mix. Although this approach may seem slightly more complicated than that used in Cubase, it's a little more flexible, as it's possible to connect two or more send effects in series by placing them in consecutive insert slots in the group channel. It's also more reflective of the way in which hardware mixers handle aux sends and returns. Figure 2.2 shows how the aux sends are set up in Logic Audio.

stereo effects

VST effects tend to come in different versions depending on whether they are required for use in a mono or stereo track. The three possibilities are mono-

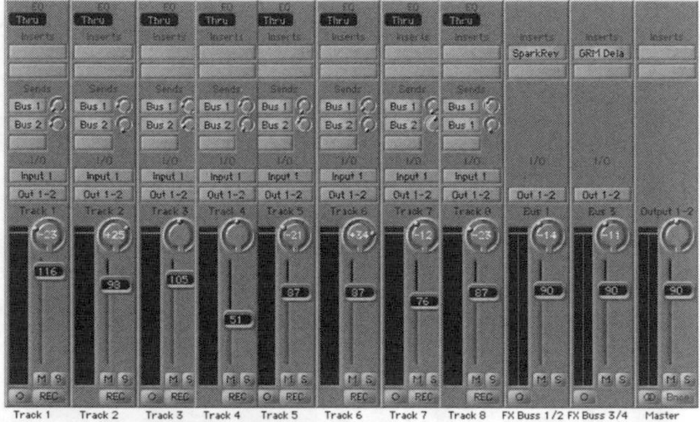

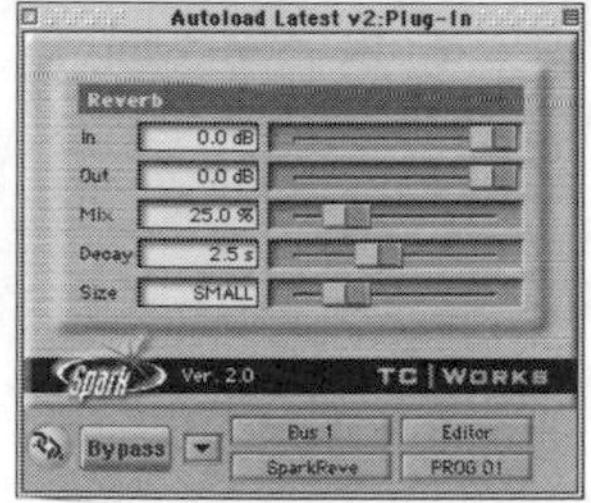

Figure 2.2: Aux sends in Logic Audio

in/mono-out, mono-in/stereo-out and stereo-in/stereo-out. As a general rule, a VST-compatible program will only allow you to see and load those versions that are appropriate for the point in the signal chain at which you're trying to use the effect. For example, if you're working in Logic Audio and you're inserting a VST effect into a stereo group for use with an aux send, you'll only be able to access stereo-in/stereo-out or mono-in/stereo-out plug-ins. Mono plug-ins will be greyed out or removed from the list, depending on the software you're using.

insert points

The other standard way to connect either effects or processors is via insert points, which can be found in the main input channels, the busses and the master stereo channel. Be aware, however, that not all software provides insert points in all of these places; simpler packages may provide inserts only in the main mixer channels.

An insert point provides a means of breaking into a signal path so that the signal can be routed via the effect or processor. The plug-in can therefore only affect what is passing through that particular channel or group, unless it's connected to the main stereo master channel, in which case the entire mix goes via the plug-in. If the plug-in is bypassed, however, the signal will pass through unchanged, just as if the plug-in wasn't there.

Most of the better-quality software on the market allows

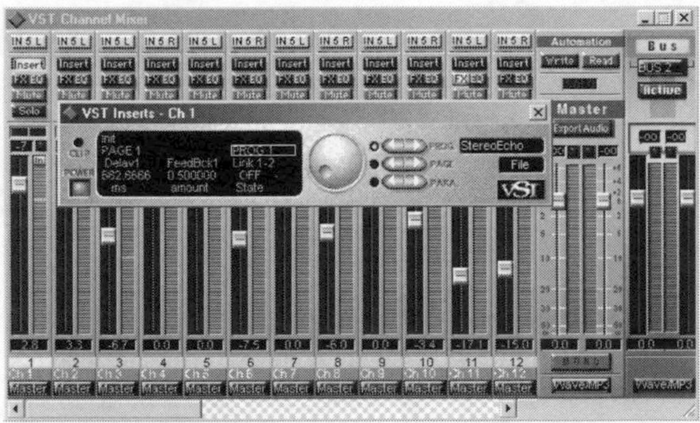

Figure 2.3: Inserts in Cubasis VST

several insert points to be opened up in the same signal path, in which case several effects or processors can be connected in series. For example, Figure 2.3 shows an insert point being set up in Cubasis. Note that, as a rule, mono-in/mono-out plug-ins should be used in mono channels, while stereo-in/stereo-out plug-ins should be used in stereo channels. However, some software is arranged so that you can insert mono-in/stereo-out plug-ins into mono channels, in which case the plug-in output should remain in stereo, even though the channel input is mono. As a rule, if a plug-in is visible in the menu, it can be used.

Figure 2.4 shows how the inserts are configured in

Logic Audio. A free plug-in slot always opens up below the ones currently being used, until the maximum number of plug-ins supported by the software is reached. The name of each plug-in is shown in the corresponding insert point, and double-clicking on the name will open up the plug-in's front panel for editing purposes.

equalisation

Depending on the type of virtual mixer, the equaliser may be built into the mixer as well as being available as a separate plug-in. For example, Cubase and Cubasis

Figure 2.4: Inserts in Logic Audio

VST provide a basic parametric EQ in each mixer channel, while in Logic Audio you have to insert an EQ plug-in if you want to use one. More sophisticated EQ plug-ins can always be used if the basic EQ isn't adequate for a particular task, but the more channels of EQ you run, the more CPU power will be needed. EQ is a processor, not an effect, and is normally used in the mixer input channels, although it may also be used in the group and master channels.

The most basic form of studio equaliser is the shelving equaliser. With these devices, a low-pass shelving filter passes all frequencies below its cut-off frequency but attenuates all frequencies above this frequency. Similarly, a high-pass filter passes all frequencies above its cut-off frequency but affects all frequencies below it. Simple shelving filters typically have a slope of 6dB per octave so that their influence is felt more progressively, although it's possible to have a filter with a much steeper slope, if required. The gentler the slope of the filter, the more frequencies outside the range of the filter will be affected.

bandpass filters

A filter that passes frequencies between two limits is known as a *bandpass filter*. On a typical sweep equaliser, the bandpass filter will have variable cut and boost controls and will also be tunable, so that its centre frequency can be varied. Sweep equalisers are more specific than shelving equalisers in that they can be tuned to the exact frequency range that needs cutting or boosting.

parametric EQ

A parametric EQ is very similar to a sweep EQ, except that a third control is added to allow the width of the filter response to be adjusted. The width of a filter response is sometimes described as its *Q value*, where Q is the frequency of the filter divided by its bandwidth. A high Q value corresponds with a very narrow filter, whereas a low Q value corresponds with a wide filter. High Q values are useful for picking out sounds that occupy a very narrow part of the audio spectrum, whereas lower Qs produce a smoother, more musical sound. Figure 2.5a shows a shelving filter response, while Figure 2.5b shows the curves produced by a typical parametric equaliser.

busses

Each mixer channel is controlled by a fader, after which the signal is routed to one or more mix busses. The

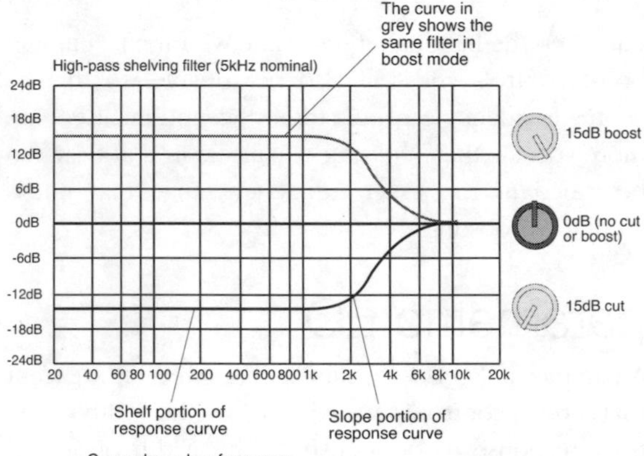

Figure 2.5: Both shelving and parametric EQ curves

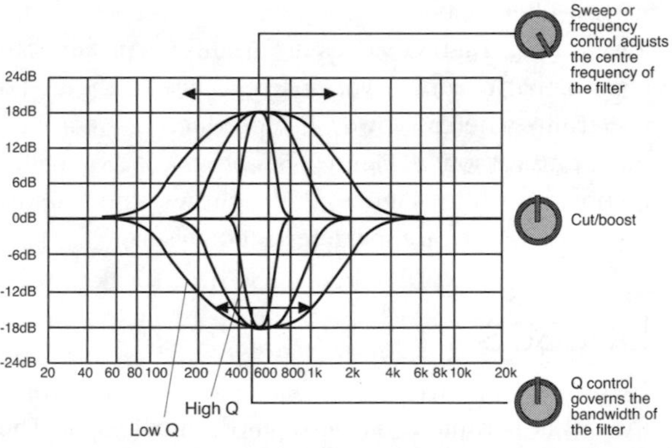

main mix buss is the stereo left/right buss, but you'll often find additional busses that can be routed either to separate physical outputs on your soundcard or that can be submixed into the main stereo buss. Busses that can be routed into the stereo mix buss are often known as *groups*.

By using the busses, you could send a different signal or mix of signals to all eight outputs of an eight-output soundcard feeding an external hardware mixer. In this case, if two or more channels are routed to the same buss, they are automatically mixed together. The channel faders still set the relative levels of the various signals being mixed, however, while the buss fader controls the overall group mix level.

You may be wondering why it's also possible to route busses back into the main stereo mix. Imagine that you have a drum kit recorded over four or five tracks of your multitrack tape. Without busses, in order to change the overall level of the kit, you'd have to move several channel faders at once. A more effective approach is to create a subgroup of the drum tracks by routing the drum channels to a stereo buss rather than directly to the left/right mix buss. This will allow you to control the level of the whole drum mix by moving just the group (buss) fader, thus making the mix much easier to manipulate.

In a typical mix, you might create subgroups from things like drums, percussion and backing vocals, which would reduce the number of faders that needed to be moved during the mix. (Note that any effects that are applied to the individual channels being grouped in this way – ie using the channel aux sends – should be returned to the same subgroup, rather than to the stereo master, if this is allowed by your mixer, or the effect level won't change when the group fader is moved.) Normally, you'd need the levels of effects such as delay and reverb to track any changes in the dry signal level. If your mixer doesn't have this option, however, you should set the group levels before adjusting the levels of effect and then refrain from adjusting the group levels any further when mixing.

automation

Console level automation is commonplace in virtual mixers, and in the case of plug-ins that conform to the VST II standard all of the plug-in parameters can be automated in the same way. However, the plug-in automation data is handled slightly differently by different software applications, so you'll need to check your user manual. When the sequencer is set to record plug-in MIDI data, any real-time changes made to the virtual plug-in controls will be recorded. On playback, these changes will be implemented at the points in the song at which they were recorded.

The most obvious use of plug-in automation is to change levels of an effect during a song, but you may also want to make more subtle changes, such as increasing the ratio of a compressor during excessively loud vocal passages or changing the rate of a chorus effect during certain parts of a song. There are also effects that produce exciting dynamic effects, such as the GRM Tools Doppler plug-in shown in Figure 2.6.

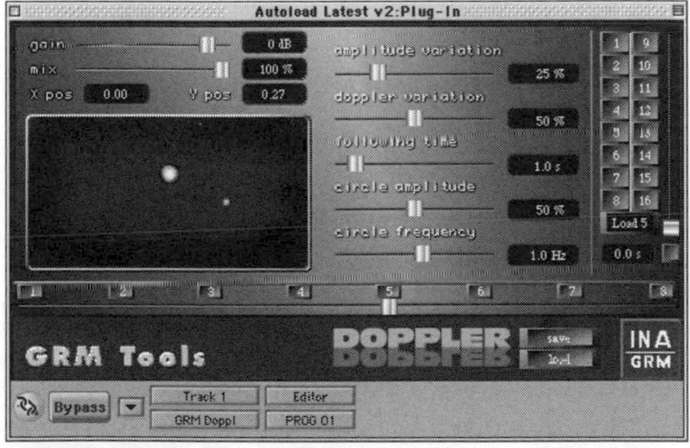

Figure 2.6: GRM Tools' Doppler plug-in

Another huge advantage of VST II plug-ins, when compared with hardware effects, is that they're able to read MIDI tempo directly from the sequencer, and many delay plug-ins make use of this by offering delay settings that are multiples of a song's tempo, rather than fixed times. In addition to simplifying the creation of tempo-related delays, these device will also allow you to set the delay time so that it automatically changes in response to a change in the song's tempo.

Note that versions of Logic Audio up to and including version 4.7 remap the MIDI controllers that are used to control VST plug-ins so that they don't conflict with Logic's own mixer automation system. However, this isn't a problem until you come to control the plug-ins from an external hardware source, when you find that the controllers that you thought would control the plug-in don't! This is slated to be resolved in Logic Audio version 5, which wasn't available at the time of writing.

gain settings

Not all audio software has the same type of data-pathway structure, which means that you have to take more care over signal levels with some programs than you do with others. As a rule, you should ensure that the highest aux send settings are around three-quarters full scale and then adjust the level of the effect being returned into the mix (where a control is provided for this purpose) in order to get the right amount of effect. By doing this, you'll minimise noise and distortion and, hopefully, keep the signal level low enough to avoid distortion. If any of the meters in your virtual mixer show the signal level to be high enough to cause clipping, locate the source of the problem and reduce the preceding levels accordingly. As always, the best situation is to have the levels as high as possible while avoiding clipping. If you can hear clipping but the meters seem happy, adjust the levels downwards and see if the problem goes away. Meters have been known to be wrong, even virtual ones!

TC Works Spark

TC Works Spark (Macintosh only) supports VST plug-ins as well as its own built-in Spark plug-ins. However, unlike other multitrack programs, which tend to use aux sends and insert points, TC Works' Spark has an effects matrix called the FX Machine that enables multiple plug-ins to be connected in various serial, parallel or serial-parallel combinations. The default matrix size is four plug-ins wide by five plug-ins long, but it can be expanded (if there's sufficient processing power available) to handle all of the plug-ins that you wish to include. Any VST or Spark plug-in can be opened in any "cell" within the matrix, and the program automatically creates parallel feeds when different plug-ins are located in the same row. Thru connections can be placed in any cell, and the outputs from cells are automatically mixed if, for example, two or more plug-ins arranged in parallel are followed by a single plug-in. Figure 2.7 shows a number of plug-ins loaded into the Spark matrix. The output levels from individual plug-ins can also be adjusted, while the side of the box around each plug-in cell also doubles as a level meter.

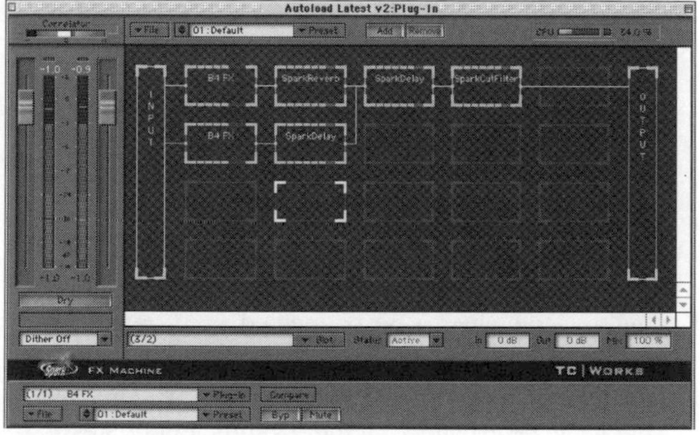

Figure 2.7: Spark FX Machine

Spark FX Machine

TC Works Spark is special in that any effect/processor combinations created in the FX Machine's matrix can be exported to any other VST- or Mark Of The Unicorn's MAS-compatible program as a single unit. In other words, the whole FX Machine set-up appears as a single plug-in. An FX Machine macro can combine true VST plug-ins with Spark's own plug-ins, and when you double click on the FX Machine plug-in name to open its control panel, the FX Machine section is displayed exactly as it appears in Spark – ie you can edit individual plug-ins conventionally without first having to open the Spark program.

Spark's VST plug-ins folder must be made available to the VST software you're using either via a dialogue box that asks which VST plug-ins folder should be used or by placing an alias/shortcut in the "VstPlugins" folder of the program you're using. Consult your software manual if you're not sure how to do this, as different programs use slightly different methods.

Once everything's set up, the next time you look down the list of VST plug-ins available to your VST program you'll find Spark FX Machine listed amongst them. From this option, you can then call up previously saved FX Machine presets or you can save new ones. Note, however, that you can only use the Spark FX Machine on a computer that has Spark loaded and authorised to run. Otherwise, both the FX Machine and any VST plug-ins that come with Spark will be inaccessible.

power shortage?

Powerful though modern computers are, there may come a time when you can't run all of the VST plug-ins you'd like to at the same time. To get around this problem, some VST-compatible software allows you to record tracks via a plug-in so that the effect is recorded, rather than applied while mixing. However, you'll need to be using a system with very low latency for this to work properly, and you'll also have to get the amount of effect right as you record, because there's no way to change it afterwards.

A safer option is to add a VST effect to an already recorded track and then to re-record the effected track as a new audio track. Fortunately, most sequencing software provides a simple way of doing this – for example, Emagic's Logic Audio has a "Bounce To Disk" function that allows one or more tracks and their effects to be mixed and bounced down to a new mono or stereo track in a single operation. Cubase does a similar thing using the audio mixer's Export function.

chapter 3

plug-in effects

The development of audio software that can use virtual plug-ins for effects and signal processing has opened up the world of serious recording to musicians working within a restricted budget and who may have never used the hardware counterparts on which today's plug-ins are based. Although plug-in effects and instruments tend to have fewer controls and adjustable parameters than high-end professional hardware, this isn't always the case, and in any event, some understanding of what the original hardware devices were designed to achieve is essential if plug-ins are to be used at all effectively.

software plug-ins

Software plug-ins can provide all of the common studio effects plus numerous esoteric functions that may not be practical to manufacture in hardware form. More new plug-ins are being made available every month, but even the more commonplace effects can be confusing if you've never used them before. The aim of this chapter isn't to provide a comprehensive overview of every VST plug-in available but rather to examine the key types of studio effects and processors and their applications, as well as to provide some practical tips concerning their use.

the plug-in interface

VST plug-ins score by having the ability to utilise as much of the computer's screen and keyboard as necessary as a user interface, whereas the hardware interface may be restricted to a small LCD window and cursor keys. A well-designed plug-in interface provides controls that can be adjusted by using a mouse in connection with graphical readouts and meters. For example, you may find dynamic graphical displays of compressor slopes or EQ curves that would be prohibitively costly to include in a hardware version.

Plug-in designers often strive to emulate the appearances of hardware boxes, so many plug-ins come equipped with elaborate computer-generated 3D representations of hardware front panels, complete with switches, knobs, faders and LEDs. Sometimes their graphical efforts are taken to extremes, but in most cases the results are clear user interfaces that are pleasant to work with. The way in which the controls are moved will vary from one manufacturer to another, but clicking on a control and then holding the mouse button down while moving the mouse will soon reveal the intended method of working. Mostly, the familiar click-and-drag system is used.

Virtually all VST plug-ins include the ability to save and reload settings, which makes it easy to build up a library of effects and processes for future use. You may also find that the designer has included a selection of factory settings to get you started. You'll also find a bypass button, although you should be aware that most effects still suck on CPU power, even when bypassed. If you don't need an effect, set the insert point or aux send to "no effect" rather than bypass the plug-in that's currently loaded.

reverberation

Reverberation is arguably the most important effect in the studio, as it mimics a very familiar aspect of our real-life environment. However, it's also one of the most processor hungry, due to the complex nature of the calculations needed to approximate what happens in a real acoustic space. Natural reverberation occurs whenever sound is reflected and re-reflected from walls and other obstacles within a large room or other acoustic space, and as we're seldom far away from a solid surface we hear natural reverb most of the time. In fact, it may surprise you to know that, in a typical concert hall, more than 90% of what you hear is reflected sound, with the direct sound from the instruments actually comprising quite a small proportion of the overall acoustic energy reaching your ears.

Each time sound encounters a surface, some of the energy is reflected and some is absorbed. Hard surfaces tend to reflect all frequencies quite efficiently, while other surfaces will absorb more high frequencies than low frequencies. It's for this reason that the physical composition of walls and other obstructions affects the tonal quality and decay time of reverberations, as does the physical spacing of the walls relative to the sound source and the listener. Because our brains rely on this complex information to make estimations concerning the type of environment in which we're listening to the sound, we can readily hear the difference between small tiled bathrooms producing long reverb times and large concert halls, even though the overall reverb time might be the same.

An electronic reverb unit mimics natural reverberation by generating thousands of closely spaced reflections (or echoes) electronically, and Figure 3.1 shows the

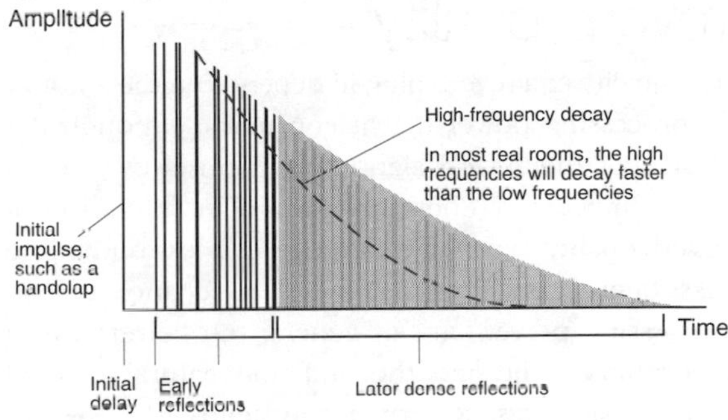

Figure 3.1: Reverb decay pattern

pattern of decaying reflections created by a typical digital reverberation unit. By varying the spacing and tonal content of these delays, artificial reverb can be used to create impressions of many different types of real room or acoustic space, but they can also be employed to create new effects that have no obvious counterpart in nature, such as impossibly long reverb times. As a rule, rooms with hard surfaces produce a bright, lively reverb sound, while more absorbent rooms produce a warmer sound with much less high end. Wood panelling actually absorbs bass energy while reflecting high frequencies quite efficiently, but in large spaces the high-frequency content of the reverberant sound soon falls away, due to absorption by the air itself.

reverb quality

The quality of a reverb plug-in depends on the amount of processing power that it consumes, although the design of the reverb algorithms themselves is even more important. Some plug-ins offer a choice of reverb quality, allowing you to opt for a less refined (ie less dense) effect if you need to economise on processing power, and in general the better reverb algorithms sound smoother and more natural than the more basic ones. Reverb quality tends to show up most on vocals and drums, and my test for overall reverb quality is to remove as much of the dry sound as possible and then listen to make sure that the result is still believable. You'll find that the better reverbs just push the apparent direct source further away as you reduce the dry sound contribution, whereas poor algorithms will sound indistinct and disembodied when the dry sound is removed.

The majority of musical applications require a fairly short reverb time of between one and three seconds, even though most reverb plug-ins can also emulate much larger reflective spaces with decay times of ten seconds or more. (You should save these more extreme settings for special effects.) Plate settings, meanwhile, are popular for general vocals and drum processing. (The term *plate* refers in this case to the mechanical reverb plate that was used in studios before digital electronics became affordable.)

Reverb plug-ins generally have stereo outputs, even if they have mono inputs, because reverberation in real life creates an impression of space and stereo width, even though the original sound may come from a single point in a room. Each ear picks up a slightly different pattern of reverb reflections, and these inter-aural differences provide information concerning spatial relationships that is used by our brains to estimate the size and character of a space. Digital reverb units can process a mono input to produce two different sets of synthetic reflections in order to create a convincing stereo effect where the two sets of reflection patterns are quite chaotic. For this reason, many VST reverb plug-ins are able to operate in a mono-in/stereo-out mode.

reverb parameters

The key reverb parameters are pre-delay time, early reflection pattern and level, overall decay time and high-frequency damping. Pre-delay relates to the time between the original sound and the first reverb reflection reaching the listener, and if you ignore reflections from the floor (which always tends to be the same distance away), a long pre-delay time suggests a large acoustic space.

Plug-ins usually offer a limited range of synthetic room types based on early patterns designed to approximate rooms, halls, chambers, plates and sometimes small-room ambience. A pre-delay control effectively delays the onset of reverb after the original sound, while the overall reverb decay time parameter (ie the time it takes for the reverb to die away) affects how we perceive the reflectivity of the environment. Longer reverb times suggest very reflective spaces, and if the reverb sound is bright, with a very short pre-delay, we might interpret this as a sound produced in a tiled room or a small cave. Longer pre-delays coupled with a less bright sound suggest larger spaces, such as a concert hall or cathedral, and in very large spaces the first few reflections may be individually audible before the complexity of the reverb merges all of the reflections together. High-frequency damping allows the high-frequency decay time to be made shorter than the overall decay time, simulating both materials that absorb high frequencies and the effect of air absorption in large spaces.

By selecting the appropriate type of reverb for the environment you wish to simulate and then adjusting the other parameters, you can create just about any acoustic environment imaginable. However, as I mentioned earlier, most of the musically useful reverb treatments have a decay time below three seconds. Longer reverb times are used mainly to create special effects.

More sophisticated algorithms may include a control that adjusts several parameters simultaneously to mimic certain sizes of room, thus saving time and making it easier for the less experienced user to set up. There may also be some form of graphical readout to show how the effect changes when the parameters are adjusted. Figure 3.2 shows a typical reverb plug-in window in TC Works' Native Reverb.

Note that well-designed, processor-efficient, low-density reverbs can still sound extremely good, most often when used with non-percussive sounds, such as

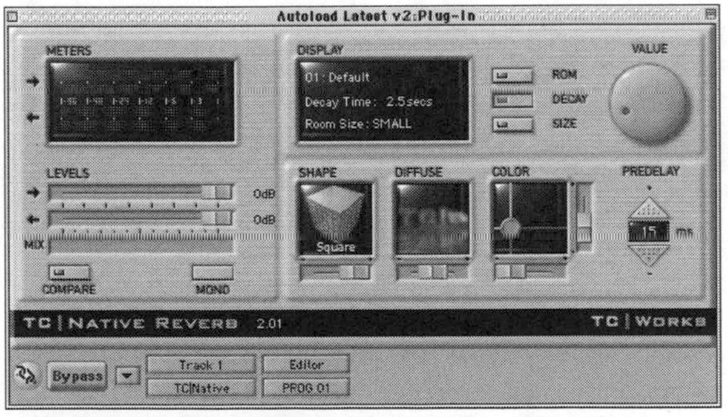

Figure 3.2: TC Works' Native Reverb plug-in

vocals, flutes, string pads and so on. Percussive sounds, on the other hand, need a dense reverb if you don't want the individual reflections to sound too obvious.

gated reverb

Gated and reverse reverb effects are common in hardware form, although they're sometimes presented as VST plug-ins. Gated reverb features an abrupt cut-off rather than a smooth decay and is created by generating a burst of closely spaced reflections, at a more or less constant level, that stop abruptly after around half a second. This effect doesn't occur in nature but is popular for creating very big, powerful drum sounds where the spaces between beats aren't filled with conventional reverb decay. It also works well on electric guitar and can even be effective on vocals, so if you have a gated reverb plug-in, try it on everything you can and see what you can create with it. Figure 3.3 shows a gated reverb envelope.

reverse reverb

When analogue tape was popular in studios, it was always fun to record something and then hear what it sounded like played backwards. Reverse reverb is very eerie indeed, and it can be approximated by using a

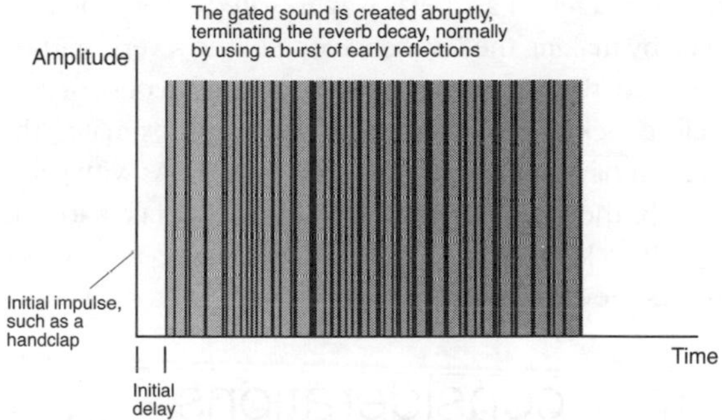

Figure 3.3: Gated reverb pattern

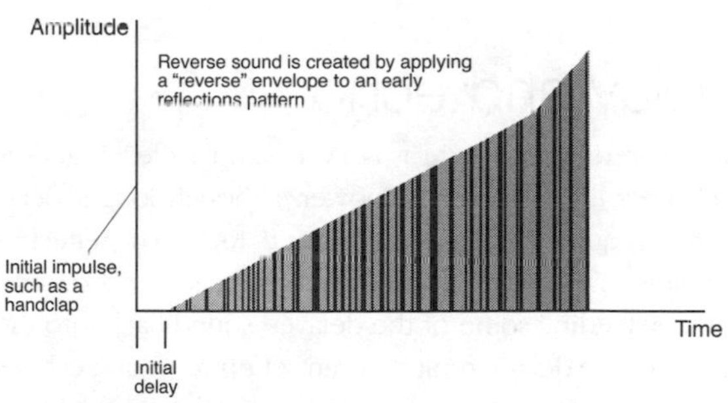

Figure 3.4: Reverse reverb pattern

digital plug-in in a similar way to gated reverb, but this time by making the level envelope of the reverb start off low and then increase steadily over a second or two before being cut off abruptly. This approximates the illusion of a tape being played backwards. As with gated reverb, the main parameter is the time it takes for the reverb to build up and then cut off. Figure 3.4 shows a reverse reverb envelope.

other considerations

Reverb is an effect and so can be used both in the aux send/return loop and in insert points. Some reverb plug-ins have informative graphical interfaces, such as the Waves TruVerb plug-in shown in Figure 3.5. Note the representation of early reflections and later decay here.

delay and echo

Compared to reverb, delay is a very simple effect that uses relatively little processing power, although longer delay times require proportionally more RAM. The effect is broadly similar to that produced by tape-loop echo units, and by feeding some of the delayed sound back into the input of the delay circuit you can set up repeating echoes that gradually die away. The time it takes for the echoes to die away is determined by the feedback parameter.

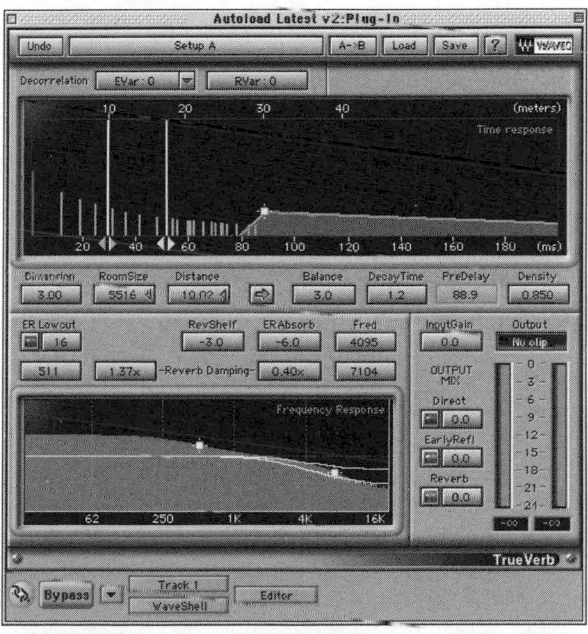

Figure 3.5: Waves' TruVerb plug-in

Some plug-ins include multitapped delay programs. The term *multitapped* means that there are several different delays occurring at once, producing an effect similar to that of a tape-loop echo unit with multiple playback heads located at different places along the tape. It may also be possible to pan the individual delays from left to right in the stereo field to create interesting spatial effects, such as ping-pong delay, where the repeats bounce from side to side. Simpler delay plug-ins are fine for creating mono or stereo delays with variable feedback, and it's also common for the delay time to be able to be linked to the tempo of the song. More complex delay units are able to generate large numbers of delay taps that behave almost like early reverb reflections, and in some cases these may be modulated to produce unusual dynamic effects, as with GRM Tools' Delays plug-in, shown in Figure 3.6. A rather different approach to multitapped delay is shown by Waves' SuperTap delay, also shown in Figure 3.6.

Simple delay plug-ins of the type described here don't sound exactly like tape-loop echo devices because they don't produce all of the unplanned side-effects of those old machines that actually conspire to make them sound very musical. For example, worn rollers can modulate the tape speed very slightly, while the limited high-frequency response of analogue tape causes each successive delay to sound gradually duller. However, the more sophisticated plug-ins imitate these side-effects, making tape-echo simulations sound more authentic.

Delay is an effect and so can be used both in the aux send/return loop and in insert points.

Figure 3.6: GRM Tools' Delays (above) and Waves' SuperTap (below) plug-ins

modulation effects

If you take a basic delay and use a low-frequency oscillator to modulate the delay time, it's possible to generate effects such as chorus, flanging, vibrato and phasing. Some modulation effects, such as phasing, use such short delay times that no delay is perceptible, while chorus and ADT use a slightly longer delay time to produce a doubling or thickening effect. While a dedicated effects box might allow you to create all of these different modulation effects by using the same delay algorithm, it's more common to present them as separate effects, and the same is true in the world of plug-ins, where chorus and flanging may be presented as quite different effects.

chorus and ADT

Chorus is created by gently modulating a short delay of around 70ms at three or four cycles per second. An equal mix of the delayed and unprocessed sound creates an effect rather like two instruments playing the same part but with slight differences in timing and tuning. With chorus, if the modulation depth is set too high, the sound takes on an unnatural warbling characteristic. Multiple delays are sometimes modulated at the same time in order to produce a richer chorus effect, and if these are panned left and right then the resulting stereo effect can be quite dramatic.

ADT (Automatic Double Tracking) is similar to chorus but uses a slightly longer delay time to create a more obvious doubling or "slapback" echo effect. ADT is often used to process vocals to make it appear that the same singer has performed the same part twice, on different tape tracks. Again, this produces a thicker sound. The amount of modulation should be so slight that it's only just noticeable.

phasing

Phasing is produced by setting up a fairly short delay of between 1ms and 10ms and then modulating the delay and mixing it with the original dry sound. Essentially, it's a little like chorus, but it uses a shorter delay time. This creates a moving comb filter (ie a filter with deep notches in its frequency response), which sounds not unlike mild tape flanging. Phasing is a popular effect for use with electric guitars and electric pianos.

flanging

Flanging was first made popular back in the psychedelic '60s. It's similar to phasing but combines slightly longer delay times (up to 50ms) with feedback in order to create a richer, more dynamic effect. The more feedback is applied, the stronger the effect. As a rule, the faster the modulation rate, the less depth you need. Flanging works well on any harmonically rich sound source. However, because it's such an obvious effect, it's best used sparingly, unless you have a good reason to do otherwise. Figure 3.7 shows the window of Waves' MetaFlanger.

vibrato

Vibrato is simply pitch modulation, and many players of acoustic string instruments – particularly guitars and violins – create vibrato by moving their fingers rapidly from side to side, changing the length of the string slightly and modulating its tension. Vibrato can be created electronically by using a modulated delay where only the delayed sound is used (ie no dry sound

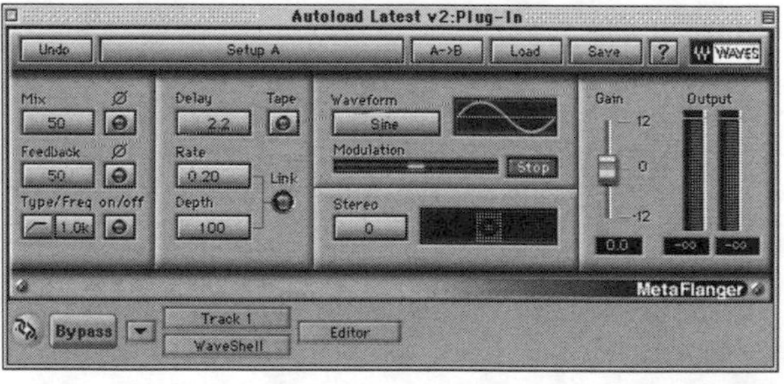

Figure 3.7: Waves' MetaFlanger plug-in

is added). The delay can be kept to just a few milliseconds so that the subjective timing of the performance isn't affected, while the intensity of the vibrato is determined by the modulation depth. A modulation rate of between two and seven cycles per second is typical. The effect is similar to using the modulation wheel on a synth. Although LFO modulation is too regular to sound natural in this respect, it still sounds musically interesting.

Because modulation effects tend to rely on a precise balance between the dry and affected sound, it's often safest to use them in insert points rather than in the effect send/return loop.

pitch shifters

Pitch shifters are designed to change the pitch of the original signal but without speeding it up or slowing it down, as is the case when you change the speed of analogue tape to create pitching effects. A similar process can be used to change the speed of a segment of audio without changing its pitch, and this is commonly known as *time stretching*, which is often used to match the tempo of drum loops or other sampled material to the rest of the song. However, whereas pitch shifting can be applied in real time,

time stretching, by its very nature, must be a non-real-time process.

Digital pitch shifting works by breaking the sound into very short segments, which are then sped up or slowed down before being joined together again. When pitching up, sections are looped to fill in the gaps that would otherwise be left between segments, while pitching down requires the segments to be truncated in order to prevent them from overlapping. With most pitch-shifting algorithms, you can hear a non-musical modulation caused by the regular modulation of the splicing process used to rejoin all of these tiny segments. The greater the pitch shift, the more noticeable the side-effects. The looping process produces a slight delay, but this can be as short as just a few milliseconds and shouldn't be musically significant.

When added to the original sound, lesser degrees of pitch shift sound very similar to chorus effects but without the regular tell-tale modulation of chorus. Pitch detuning of just a few "cents", combined with a short delay, can be used to thicken vocals or instrumental pad parts.

Because pitch shifting does have such obvious side-effects, especially if it has been designed to be economical with processing power, for more discerning work you may prefer to use your sequencer's offline pitch-shifting facility rather than a real-time VST plug-in. Offline processes are able to examine an audio file prior to processing, after which they optimise their processing to suit the material, and so the result is often more satisfactory, musically. Once everything is set up, they then produce new audio files complete with the required degrees of pitch shift, and of course the original files remain on your hard drive unchanged. If

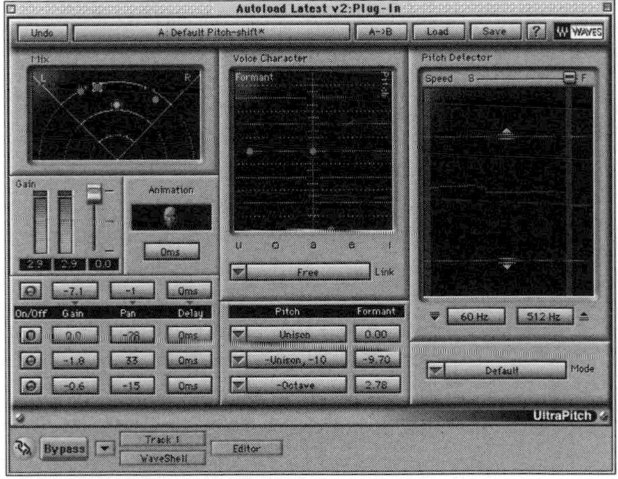

Figure 3.8: Waves' UltraPitch plug-in

you need to process loops sampled from records or taken from sample CDs, offline processing will probably produce the best results, although the side-effects of real-time pitch shifting may still be usable in a creative context. Pitch shifting is an effect and so can be used both in the aux send/return loop and insert points, although it's more commonly used via an insert point.

Figure 3.8 shows the Waves UltraPitch plug-in, which can simultaneously change both the pitch and formant frequency of a sound. In this example, three pitch-shifted signals can be produced at once and positioned at different places in the stereo field.

autopanners

An autopanner pans a mono signal from left to right in a mix, usually under the control of a low-frequency oscillator or external trigger. If controlled by an oscillator, the main user adjustment will pan the speed. Also, as I said earlier, because VST II plug-ins can be designed to read MIDI and tempo information, you may find that the pan rate can be set to a multiple of the song tempo. Tempo-synchronised panning can be quite effective, as it enhances the rhythm of a song rather than conflicts with it. Stereo versions of autopanners are also available, and these cause the two input signals to pan in opposite directions. One tip here is to try panning only the output from an effect plug-in rather than panning the entire signal, as the full effect can sometimes be overpowering.

Because autopanners tend not to use any dry signal, they should be treated as signal processors and used only in insert points. They are usually configured mono-in/stereo-out.

amp/speaker simulators

Keyboards usually sound best through a clean signal path with a flat frequency response and minimal distortion, although distortion can sometimes be used as a special effect. Guitar and bass amplifiers, on the other hand are "voiced", which means that their frequency responses are shaped to flatter the instrument. Guitar loudspeakers and enclosures also tend to have very limited frequency responses, which enables them to filter out the rougher-sounding components of amplifier distortion, which is how the sound of the traditional guitar distortion effect evolved. Guitar pre-amp plug-ins based on physical-modelling principles can emulate both amplifier distortion and amp/speaker coloration to create quite authentic electric guitar sounds, but if you don't play guitar then it's still worth trying them on synth sounds, especially bass patches or sampled drum loops.

Figure 3.9: Steinberg's Red Valve·It plug-in

Although hardware solutions may be more convenient, software guitar amps and speaker simulators have the advantage that you can record the guitar part clean and then change the amp sound after recording. Note that, if you need to hear the effect of an amp simulator plug-in in real time during performance, you'll need a system with very low latency (ie less than 7ms). Figure 3.9 shows Steinberg's Red Valve·it guitar pre-amp plug-in, which models the behaviour of a real amplifier and speaker system.

Amp simulators are processors, and so they should only

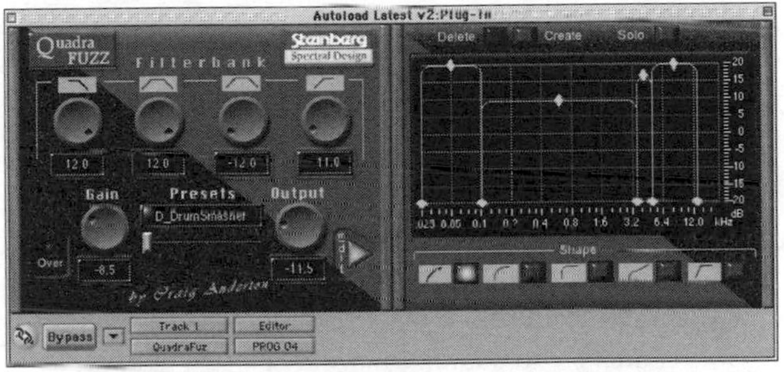

Figure 3.10: Steinberg's QuadraFuzz plug-in

be used in insert points (even if the amp models include effects).

distortion

Numerous plug-ins are available that distort sound in a more general way, either by emulating analogue saturation and clipping or by reducing the bit depth of the original audio signal. These plug-ins are popular in dance music circles for creating "lo-fi" sounds. There are also some more sophisticated distortion plug-ins available that split the audio signal into separate frequency bands and then distort each band independently, such as Steinberg's QuadraFuzz, for example (see Figure 3.10). This approach produces a more tightly controlled sound than basic overall distortion and is particularly useful for beefing up drum loops and dance synth sounds.

Distortion plug-ins that work by reducing the bit resolution of a signal produce quite nasty inter-modulation effects and noise that work well in dance music but are of little use in conventional rock or pop music. Also note that a distortion plug-in used on its own is unlikely to sound good with electric guitars, as the filtering effect produced by the loudspeaker system will be missing.

Finally, remember that distortion is a process and so should be used only in insert points.

tube emulators

Even though we live in a digital age, many musicians still like the sound of tube (also known as valve) equipment, as its technical imperfections can be very flattering when used in certain types of recording. The individual quality of the sound produced by tube equipment is largely due to subtle non-linearities that introduce harmonic distortion at higher signal levels, unlike digital electronic equipment, which produces a clean signal until it reaches the maximum possible level, after which hard clipping occurs.

Figure 3.11: DUY's DaD Valve plug-in

Different tube circuits add different types of harmonic distortion, but in a typical device, second, third and fifth harmonic distortion will be introduced in greater proportions as the signal level is increased. Paradoxically, this distortion can have the effect of making the signal seem actually brighter and cleaner than it actually is, and bass instruments also tend to sound punchier and warmer than before.

In order to bring these sonic attributes into the digital domain, engineers have spent a considerable amount of time analysing the behaviour of tube equipment at different signal levels and have created algorithms that emulate this behaviour very closely, hence a number of VST plug-ins now include tube-emulation sections, often in combination with equalisers. Clearly, tube emulation is a process and should be used in an insert point, not in an aux send. Figure 3.11 shows the DUY DaD Valve plug-in, which aims to emulate the sonic characteristics produced by a classic valve circuit.

filters

In addition to parametric and graphic equalisers, there are plug-ins available that can emulate the swept-resonant filters used in synthesisers. These may be controlled via an LFO, via the level of the input signal or sometimes via their own MIDI-triggered envelope. Any audio signal can be treated, from basic keyboard sounds to drums and vocals. The usual controls are cut-off frequency, resonance and modulation depth, although it's also common to be able to switch the type of the filter between low-pass, bandpass and high-pass settings. More sophisticated plug-ins may offer different filter slopes, usually from 6dB per octave to 24dB per octave. The purposes of these different slopes is to enable the filter to emulate more accurately the filter sections of various classic

Figure 3.12: TC Works' TouchWah plug-in

synthesisers. Simpler filters may be configured as guitar wah-wah pedals, such as TC Works' TouchWah, shown in Figure 3.12.

Finally, it's important to remember that filters are processors, and so they should only be connected via insert points.

compressors/limiters

Compressors are among the most important signal processors used in the studio, so it's worth spending a little time to understand them properly. They're often used to "even out" excessive peaks in signal level that occur in vocal or instrumental performances by automatically changing the gain of the signal path in response to the level of the signal passing through the compressor. In other words, a compressor reduces the dynamic range of an audio signal by reducing the difference between the quietest passages and the loudest.

Compressors work by reducing the gain of signals that occur above a threshold set by the user, so that louder signals are made quieter while signals falling below the threshold remain unchanged. The degree of gain reduction is determined by the compression ratio parameter – the higher the ratio, the more the signals exceeding the threshold level are reduced. The ratio is calculated as the number of decibels by which the compressor input must be increased to produce a 1dB increase in output level. An example of a compressor plug-in, the Waves C1, is shown in Figure 3.13.

At very high ratio values, a compressor's maximum output is maintained at the threshold level and is effectively prevented from going beyond it, and this is a process known as *limiting*. Limiting is used in circumstances where it would be undesirable for a signal to exceed a specific level – for example, to prevent clipping on a digital recorder. However, a high ratio on its own is no guarantee that all peaks will be brought under control, as a compressor's attack parameter determines how quickly the circuitry responds once a signal has exceeded the threshold. Unless the attack time is very fast, it's possible for short peaks to escape gain reduction, as the compressor won't respond fast enough. The attack

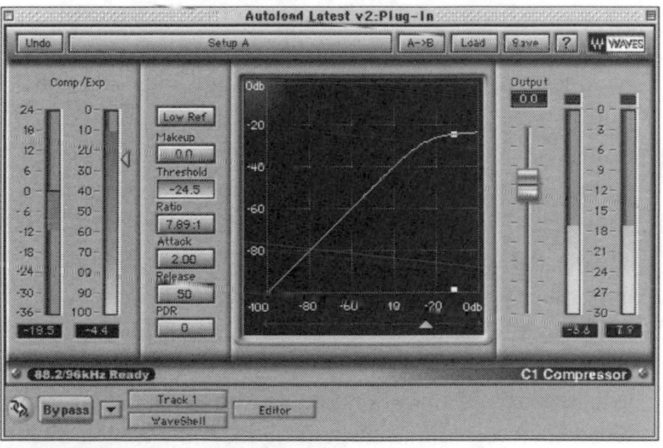

Figure 3.13: Waves' C1 Compressor plug-in

time is made adjustable because some types of audio material sound better when processed with a longer attack time – for example, drums and other percussive sounds can sound more lively if the start of the sound is allowed to pass through the compressor before gain reduction is applied.

The release parameter sets the time it takes for the gain to return to normal once the input has dropped back below the threshold setting. Some compressors have auto-attack and -release settings that respond to the dynamic characteristics of input signals, and Auto mode is very useful when it comes to processing signals with constantly changing sonic characteristics, such as vocal lines, slap/pull bass guitar or even complete mixes.

Compressors designed for use with stereo signals include two separate signal channels that have their side-chain circuits linked so that both channels are always compressed by the same amount. This is necessary to prevent the image from appearing to move to one side or the other when a loud sound appears on only one side of the mix, and this happens in a way that's undetectable to the user. When you select a stereo compressor plug-in, the two channels will automatically be linked.

Digital plug-ins, such as compressors, have the added advantage that they can "look ahead" and see what signal peaks are coming and so can react more promptly. Not all compressor plug-ins have this facility, however, and in some cases those that do have it can have the function switched off in order to produce a sound that's more similar to that produced by an analogue compressor.

Because compressors reduce the levels of signal peaks, it's sometimes necessary to increase the gain of a compressor's output to restore the signal level. This is done by using a "make up gain" or "output gain" control, which may have associated metering to prevent the signal level from being increased too far. Once the output gain has been adjusted, the compressor will effectively be increasing the level of quiet sounds at the same time as it controls the levels of peaks. This means that any low-level noise present in the input signal will also be boosted, so it may be beneficial to patch a gate or expander plug-in before the compressor to make sure that any pauses are completely silent.

Finally, remember that compressors are signal processors and so should only be used in insert points.

gates

Whereas compressors control the levels of high-level signals, gates control the levels of signals that fall below a threshold set by the user. The purpose of a gate is to silence a signal during pauses, when any background noise won't be masked by the presence of a signal. If the threshold level of a gate is set just above the background noise, the gate will operate whenever there is a pause in the signal.

Like compressors, most gates have attack and release times that can be adjusted to produce the most natural results on the material being processed. Without these controls, gates would always open and close abruptly, producing an unnaturally clipped sound. As a rule, fast attack sounds require a fast gate attack setting, while slowly decaying sounds need a slow release to prevent the end of the wanted sound from being cut off abruptly. Sounds that have a naturally slow attack may sound smoother if the attack time of the gate is set slightly slower.

It should be understood that gates only remove noise when there's a pause in the wanted signal. They can't remove noise that's audible over the top of the programme material. Figure 3.14 shows the Waves C1 Gate/Expander plug-in.

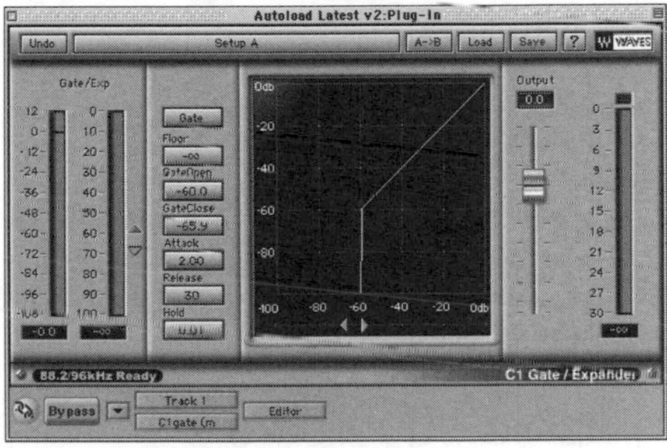

Figure 3.14: Waves' C1 Gate/Expander plug-in

expanders

Expanders are very similar to gates, with the exception that, when the signal falls below the threshold, they close down gently according to a ratio set by the user, much like a compressor in reverse. An expander with a very high ratio behaves in exactly the same way as a gate, while a lower ratio setting serves to reduce the level of signals falling below the threshold rather than muting them entirely.

Both gates and expanders are signal processors and should be used only in insert points.

equalisers

Parametric and shelving equalisers were discussed in the previous chapter, and combinations of these types of equaliser often form the basis of equaliser plug-ins. Equalisers are used both to correct tonal faults and to enhance sounds. Because of the way in which the human ear detects sound, EQ cut is less intrusive than EQ boost, especially when narrow sections of the audio spectrum are involved.

graphic equalisers

A hardware graphic equaliser can be recognised by the row of faders across its front panel, and plug-ins tend to mimic this layout, where each of these faders controls a narrow section of the audio spectrum. Other than the highest and lowest faders, which control shelving filters, each of the filters in a graphic equaliser is a fixed-frequency bandpass filter by which boost is applied by moving the fader up from its centre position and cut is achieved by moving the fader down. Figure 3.15 shows the visual display and user interface of the TC Works Native EQ plug-in, which, as you can see, is much like that of a hardware graphic equaliser.

Graphic equalisers have the advantage of being very easy to set up, but they're also less flexible than the

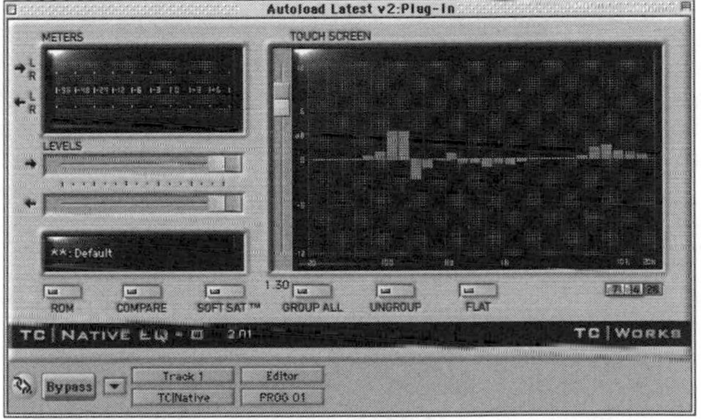

Figure 3.15: TC Works' Native EQ plug-in

parametric EQ, which can be exactly tuned to specific frequencies. Some EQ plug-ins provide multiple bands of adjustment, like a hardware graphic equaliser, and often display frequency-response curves so that the combined effect of the various filter controls can be clearly seen.

A further refinement is the paragraphic equaliser, on which each band of a multiband equaliser has full parametric controls in addition to a cut/boost slider. These controls combine the visual representation of a graphic equaliser with the flexibility of a parametric equaliser they are particularly useful in mastering applications.

Equalisers are processors and so must be connected via insert points rather than via aux sends.

enhancers

Enhancers are devices that add synthesised high-frequency harmonics to signals by using filtering, controlled distortion and compression, making a track sound brighter and more "up front". The original exciter process was developed and patented by Aphex, although there are now several different approaches to enhancement, all of which work on slightly different principles. Enhancement is quite different to equalisation, because EQ can only boost harmonics that already exist. It's no use boosting the high end if there is no high end to boost, as all you'll do is increase the level of noise. Enhancement, on the other hand, actually synthesises a new high end based on musical information that exists at lower frequencies and so is able to add a musically realistic top end to signals that were originally lacking in high-frequency content.

Enhancers are used to push sounds to the front of a mix or to create clarity and space in crowded mixes. They can also be used to brighten up old recordings, although noisy material may sound even more cluttered after enhancement. There are various exciter plug-ins available, although they should be used with care, as it's easy to make a mix or track sound harsh by over-processing it.

Enhancers are processors and so should be used in an insert point rather than in an aux send, even though the enhancement process involves mixing the dry signal with the harmonically synthesised signal.

pitch correctors

It has long been the dream of studio engineers to have a magic box capable of correcting pitching errors in vocals, and at the end of the 20th century the USA-based company AnTares came up with a hardware device that could do just that. Shortly afterwards, they released a VST plug-in version. AnTares Auto-Tune provides a practical answer to the very real problem of vocal pitching imperfections, so it isn't surprising that other companies are already developing competing products.

Auto-Tune works by first calculating the pitch of an incoming signal, and so it can only work with monophonic sources. Once the pitch has been detected, it is compared with the actual pitches of the notes in the musical scale that will be used in the song. Auto-Tune then uses real-time pitch-shifting techniques to change the pitch of the original sound to match the nearest note in the scale. Any scale or sequence of notes can be entered by the user, and it's also possible to leave Auto-Tune set to a chromatic scale. However, in this case, a badly sung note might be closer to the next semitone above or below the target note, in which case the pitch-correction system will actually compound the error. Because of this, it's always best to enter a target scale, if possible, especially if the singer has serious pitching problems.

Using Auto-Tune is very simple, considering the spectacular results that can be achieved. An on-screen slider adjusts the ratc at which pitch correction takes place, and so, by slowing down the reactions of the program, natural bends and vibrato are allowed through unaltered. Setting the pitch correction to its fastest setting produces a very unnatural pitch-quantisation effect that was first exploited on Cher's single 'Believe'.

Although the main function of Auto-Tune is to tighten up vocal pitching, it can also be used to produce creative effects and to improve performances on monophonic instrument. Even sounds like fretless bass, cello, violin and lead guitar can be pitch corrected without losing their essential characteristics, although it's important to experiment with the pitch-correction speed to achieve the most natural-sounding results.

Pitch-correction plug-ins are processors and so must always be patched in via an insert point to treat a single monophonic sound source.

bass enhancers

Typical compact home hi-fi systems can't produce the lowest fundamental frequencies of bass guitars, kick drums or electronic bass instruments. However, because of the human brain's ability to compensate for missing information, they can still sound quite impressive. It's also possible to process audio signals so that they sound even better on this kind of playback system.

One such system works by doubling the frequencies of those fundamentals that are too low for small loudspeakers to reproduce while at the same time reducing the level of these original low fundamentals. MaxxBass from Waves works in this way. By reducing the genuine low bass content and increasing the level of the newly generated harmonics, the signal can actually be made to sound as though it has more bass

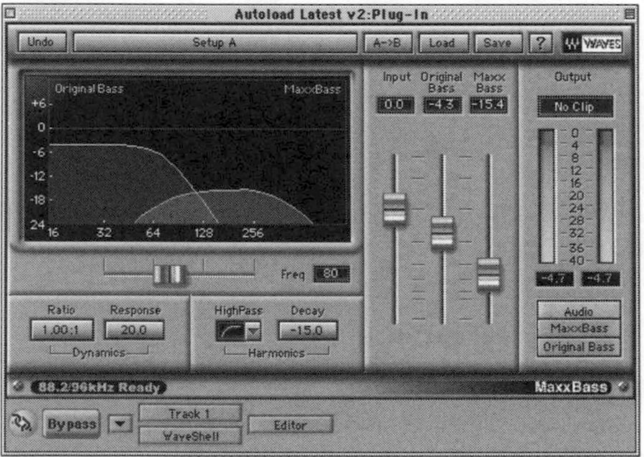

Figure 3.16: Waves' MaxxBass plug-in

energy when played back over small speakers. Also, because the low-frequency energy has been reduced, there's less stress on the speakers, enabling them to play louder before distortion becomes a problem.

Although such bass-enhancement plug-ins are seldom used for commercial music releases, they are extremely useful when producing music for computer games or other multimedia applications where the end speaker system is likely to have a limited low-end frequency response. The aforementioned Waves MaxxBass plug-in is shown in Figure 3.16.

Bass-enhancement plug-ins are processors and so may be used via insert points. However, they can be used to treat complete mixes as well as single sound sources, if used via a buss of stereo master insert point.

stereo-width enhancers

Conventional enhancers work on the frequency spectrum of the sound being processed to make it sound brighter or more punchy, but there are other processes available that can be applied to increase the sense of stereo width of material destined to be played back over stereo speakers. Indeed, some systems claim to be able to create the illusion or surround sound, where some sounds seem to come from behind the listening position.

A very simple way of expanding stereo width is to take some of the information in the right channel, phase-invert it and then add it to the left channel. Likewise, some of the left channel information is phase-inverted and added to the right channel. This pushes the apparent stereo width of the mix outwards beyond the limits of the speakers. This process is also mono compatible (ie the added signals cancel out in mono). However, it isn't possible to position sounds to the extreme sides or behind the listener in this way.

Systems that are able to do this are much more sophisticated and rely on psycho-acoustic processing.

Probably the best-known systems for psycho-acoustic positioning are Q Sound, Roland's RSS system and Spatializer. All rely on the fact that the human brain perceives sound direction by comparing the sounds that arrive at both ears. Small differences in arrival time and tonality due to the listener's position are subconsciously analysed to establish the direction of the sound source, and by artificially manipulating these parameters it's sometimes possible to fool the brain into thinking that a sound is coming from somewhere other than the actual source. The difference in tonality when sound approaches the head from different angles is due to both the shape of the outer ear and the way in which the head itself masks or shadows sounds coming from the opposite side. By using filters and delays to recreate the conditions that occur when a sound comes from the side or from behind, it's possible to greatly increase the sense of sound-source position, even though the sound is really coming from a pair of stereo speakers somewhere in front of the listener.

A number of stereo-width-enhancement processes are available as VST plug-ins, sometimes in combination with other functions, although the success with which sounds can be positioned outside the loudspeakers or even behind the listener tends to depend on both the nature of the sound being processed and the accuracy and set-up of the listener's stereo speakers. Because the outcome isn't always consistent across all sound-playback systems, such effects are often used to treat only specific elements within a mix rather than the whole mix – for example, sound effects, additional percussion or the outputs from effects devices. You should also be aware that the necessary tonal changes and delays needed to create these effects inevitably compromise mono compatibility, so it always pays to listen to a mono version of the processed mix to make sure that the end result is still acceptable.

vocoders

The vocoder is one of those effects that you recognise instantly when you hear it. Put simply, it superimposes the characteristics of one sound input onto another – for example, the articulation of a human voice onto the sound of an electronic keyboard. The result is the classic talking synth sound, where the harmonic content and musical pitch are contributed by the synthesiser but are then filtered through the spectral content of the voice. Vocoders are now available as VST plug-ins, and in addition to creating talking-instrument effects it's also possible to vocode rhythm loops with synthesised sounds or to combine other unusual sources to produce interesting results.

While hardware vocoders are real-time devices, many plug-in vocoders are designed to process existing tracks or audio files. Others may include basic synth sections to provide the "carrier" signal onto which the characteristics of a vocal track are modulated.

instrument or effect?

The topic of VST instruments is covered in detail in a separate book in this series, *basic VST INSTRUMENTS*, although some of these include sophisticated effects sections that can be accessed separately for use with other audio sources. For example, VST instruments from Native Instruments often have useful effects sections that can be accessed in this way. Their excellent B4 ToneWheel organ plug-in includes a very accurately modelled rotary speaker system that also appears in VST effects lists as a separate plug-in, as shown in Figure 3.17. Rotary speakers were developed for the electric organ and work by means of using rotating loudspeaker drive units or moving baffles positioned in front of stationary loudspeaker drive units to produce an interesting chorus/vibrato effect. By

Figure 3.17: Native Instruments' B4 effects plug-in

changing the speed of the motor, the effect can vary from a lazy phasing-like treatment to a fast swirl.

The B4's simulation of rotary speakers is quite elaborate, and in addition to making it possible for you to set the speed of the effect it also models the effect of the speaker when miked at different distances and with different mic spacings. The rate at which the motor accelerates and decelerates when the Speed switch is changed can also be set independently for the high-frequency drivers (tweeters) and the bass speaker.

Obviously, the B4 rotary speaker plug-in works well on organ-style sounds, but it also produces very interesting results on electric guitars, vocals and other keyboard sounds. The Beatles were one of the first bands to really experiment with the rotary speaker cabinet in this way, and if you've never heard the effect it produces, I'd recommend that you try it, as it's very powerful and quite unlike anything you can achieve by using a flanger, phaser or chorus plug-in.

other types of plug-in

The beauty of the VST plug-in format is that designers are coming up with new ideas all the time and, unlike hardware effects, they don't need to have a whole new production line at their disposal to get their ideas onto the market. VST plug-ins can emulate vintage analogue processors or produce outrageous brand-new effects. Also, unlike hardware effect boxes, they don't wear out. For something truly weird, try out Native Instruments' Spektral Delay, shown Figure 3.18. This plug-in splits an audio signal into hundreds of separate frequency bands and then delays them all individually under the control of a simple graphical interface.

There are also plug-ins available that will add noise and crackle to a signal in order to simulate a vinyl recording.

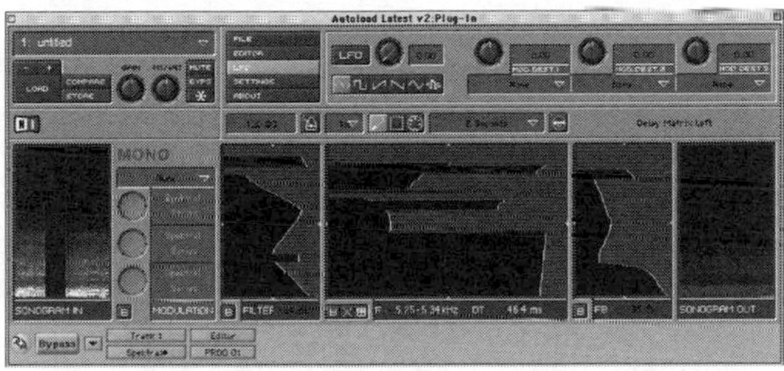

Figure 3.18: Native Instruments' Spektral Delay plug-in

These programs include such parameters as record speed, recording age and amount of surface damage. You'll also find that a large number of plug-ins are developed by enthusiasts and are made available free of charge to users via the Internet. However, it's impossible to vouch for the quality or stability of such software, and in many cases it's only available for either Mac or PC instead of both.

Plug-ins are also an ideal tool for mastering, as there are models that are capable of handling denoising, declicking, multiband compression, limiting, complex EQ and so on. Multiband dynamics processors allow the bass, mid-range and high frequencies to be processed independently, which provides a high degree of control over the way in which complete mixes can be processed. Multiband compressors and limiters tend to produce fewer audible side-effects than full-band processors, although it takes a little experience to be able to use them effectively.

MIDI control

Most of the current MIDI-plus-audio sequencers can use MIDI information to automate plug-in effect parameters, provided that both the host software and the plug-in support the full VST II plug-in specification. Exactly which parameters are available for automation is down to the designer of the plug-in, although it's not uncommon for every variable parameter to be able to be automated. However, not all plug-ins respond smoothly to real-time MIDI control, and you may hear a buzzing or rasping noise as parameters are changed. Even a well-designed plug-in may sound rough if too many parameters are changed too quickly.

chapter 4

VST mixing

When you make a recording, you'll probably build up your mix a track at a time and then set the approximate level of each part as you record them it in order to make it easier to overdub new parts. In other words, by adjusting your monitor mix as you record, you'll be setting up a balance that will be close to what you'll eventually need when you come to mix. At this stage, you probably won't have included any level-automation moves or set the panning positions for your tracks, but at least you should have a mix that sounds roughly correct.

This is a good time to patch in any VST plug-ins that you know you're going to be needing in your final mix. For example, your vocal tracks will almost certainly need compressors (via channel insert points) and you'll need at least one reverb, which should be connected via one of the aux sends. In some situations, you may need two or more reverbs of different lengths, one to suit the vocals and others for the drums and other instruments.

Personally, I feel that too many people reach for the EQ controls as a matter of course and consequently end up with strangled-sounding mixes that sound unsatisfying. EQ has its place, but I like to get an initial balance with little or no EQ first of all so that I can listen to the mix as a whole to hear what's really needed. One very important thing to learn is that sounds heard in the context of a mix sound completely different when heard in isolation, so spending ages working on a solo'd bass guitar sound, for example, is unlikely to produce the result that will work best in a final mix.

You should check effects plug-ins connected via aux sends to make sure that they have correct input levels – the meters should read about three-quarters full scale on loud passages and they shouldn't ever be allowed to clip.

working methods

Every engineer has his own way of working, and to some extent the style of music will influence his approach to a mix, too, but my own way of approaching pop and dance mixes is first to establish a good drum and bass balance. The apparent balance may change once the rest of the instruments and voices are in the mix, but getting these sounding right from the start gives you a foundation on which to start building the rest of the track.

I find that it's useful to get the lead vocal up fairly early on in the proceedings, as this will give you and idea of how much space is left for the remaining instruments. After this, the other faders can be brought up one at a time until a decent overall balance has been achieved. All too often, a musician will produce a great-sounding backing mix only to find that it's too busy to allow the vocals to sit with it comfortably. Don't hesitate to drop a part if it's making the mix too busy or to perhaps change a thick MIDI synth sound for something thinner. Only when all of the instruments are in place should you refine the EQ and balance.

Some engineers and producers insist that the best way of working is to pull up all of the faders and then adjust them until a good balance is achieved. Although this takes a little experience to get right, it's a quick way of hearing how everything works together. If you've been tweaking levels as you've been recording, you're probably not far off this point, anyway.

Before going any further, I'd suggest that you examine each of your audio tracks in turn and silence any unwanted pauses to make sure that no uninvited sounds find their way into your mix. You can use the Silence command in the audio editing section of your program to do this, or you can use the program's level-automation facilities to turn tracks down when they're not contributing to the mix. For example, you'd normally mute the vocal track whenever the singer was silent in order to prevent headphone spill, coughs and other noises finding their way onto your finished master.

If the mix requires level automation to bring up a guitar part during a solo, for example, or to bring up the occasional quiet vocal phrase that the compressors can't deal with, do this now. Even with a good preliminary mix, some parts invariably need their levels changed, but listen carefully and make sure that the level changes aren't too obvious. As a general rule, don't make large changes to the levels of drums or bass instrument, as the rhythm section needs to sound consistent. If you feel that some level control is needed, try compression instead.

producing with VST

Now that you have a reasonable balance, you can start to work on the effects and the stereo positioning of the tracks. Remember, however, that you can only use VST effects to process audio tracks and virtual instruments such as VST instruments. Your hardware MIDI instruments will either have to rely on their own internal effects or have effects added to them at the mixer via hardware effects units. Also, when sequenced MIDI instruments are being used, it's usually possible to program level changes via MIDI, but if you want to use your software's audio mixer automation or VST plug-ins to process them, you'll have record the outputs of your MIDI devices back onto the computer as audio tracks. Once they're recorded as audio, you can process them with VST plug-ins just as you can with all other audio tracks.

Assuming that you have your compressors and reverbs set up correctly, you may like to experiment with further plug-ins or even with plug-in automation. The latter is particularly effective when using resonant filters, a popular technique in dance music, although you can also add polish to a mix by bringing in delays at certain points or by increasing the level and/or decay time of a reverb at the end of a line or phrase. There are no solid rules, however, and producers of dance music are pushing the boundaries all the time, so the best advice I can give here is to take the time to listen closely to some music in the styles that interest you and try to pin down what types of effects have been applied. Once you've experimented with your plug-ins to find out what they do, you'll be surprised at how easy it is to pick out those effects on commercial records.

panning

Bass drums, bass guitars and other bass sounds are usually panned to the centre, as this provides a focus for the mix and also splits the load of these high-energy sounds to both loudspeakers. Lead vocals tend to be positioned centre-stage, because that's where the listener expects the vocalist to be. Of course, you can always choose another position, if you have an artistic reason for doing so.

Backing vocals can be panned wherever you feel they sound best, although it's usually a quite effective technique to spread them out on either side of the main vocal. If you can hear any sibilance problems, a de-esser plug-in should be patched into the vocal channel's insert point, ideally after the compressor. If you're using a bright-sounding reverb, it can help to patch a de-esser before the reverb, although not all audio software will let you "chain" plug-ins in the aux send path in this way. Anyone who owns TC Works' Spark or some other program that lets you wrap multiple VST plug-ins can use this to create a combination of plug-ins – for example, a de-esser followed by a reverb – that can be used in the main audio program as a single plug-in. This is a good way around the routing limitations of certain audio software programs.

Once you think you've got the mix about right, listen to the balance from an adjacent room with the adjoining door left open. Virtually every professional studio engineer I know swears by this technique, which shows up balance problems very clearly, even though you may have been quite unaware of them when sitting right in front of the speakers.

gates and mutes

Gates and expanders are very effective when it comes to cleaning up tracks that have some audible noise in the middle of pauses. While you can silence longer pauses by using your software's edit functions or mix automation, this often isn't practical when you're dealing with very short pauses, such as those between words or between short musical phrases. In these cases, you should use a gate or an expander plug-in. These are quite easy to set up, although you must remember to set the threshold as low as you can without the noise triggering the gate, and you must take care to match the release time of the gate to the sound being processed. Gates can only keep the noise down during pauses and can do nothing when a signal is present, but as long as you've taken reasonable care while recording, any background noise should be completely masked by the audio when the gate is open.

mix processing

You might think that, if you use compression on the tracks that need it, there would be no need to compress the final stereo mix. Certainly, this isn't obligatory, but it does often help to gel the various parts of a track together. Compressing a complete mix reduces the difference between the quietest parts of the mix and the loudest, and so, if an instrument or voice drops out of the mix, the overall level will be nudged up slightly to compensate. If you want to try this, patch a compressor plug-in into the master stereo output insert point of your virtual mixer.

When compressing a mix, the attack time of the compressor is usually extended slightly to allow transient sounds such as drums to punch through with more power, although the best setting can only be determined by ear. Some compressor plug-ins perform disappointingly when used on complete mixes, whereas others sound particularly musical, so try different compressor plug-ins to find the best one for you. Two very general rules are that soft-knee compressors produce the most subtle results and that the amount of compression you need to apply will depend on how the material will be mastered later. If you're having your material mastered professionally, it's best to apply little or no compression to the final mix, as the mastering studio will invariably have better-sounding equipment than you, so leave the job up to them. If, on the other hand, you're doing the whole job yourself, your decision will depend on whether you consider your final mix to be a master or whether you're going to work on the final mix with editing software and mastering plug-ins. If the latter is the case, the advice on using little or no mix compression still applies.

mastering with VST

For mastering purposes, multiband compressors produce the best results, as they provide a lot more control over the compression process, although they also require a little more experience to be used effectively. Most multiband compressors process audio in three bands, roughly comprising bass, mid-range and high frequencies. By applying more compression to the bass frequencies, the apparent energy of a mix can be increased without the quality of the mid-range or high-end frequencies being affecting. However, one key point to bear in mind when mastering is that, on most occasions, you'll need very low ratios (usually lower than 1.5:1) and much lower threshold settings than you would for routing single-source compression. A typical set-up might be a ratio of 1.3:1 and a threshold setting of around -30dB, producing a gain reduction of 4-6dB on the loudest peaks.

It's also common to follow the compressor with a fast peak limiter so that the signal peaks are never allowed to clip for more than a few consecutive samples. Clipping distortion only tends to be audible when it extends beyond ten consecutive samples, and most good limiter plug-ins will bring the level under control within this time. This produces a loud mix that transfers well to CD. Figure 4.1 shows the DUY MAX limiter plug-in, which is popular in mastering applications, as is the Waves L1 and TC Works' Maxit.

Equalising an entire mix can improve the sound noticeably, even when very subtle settings are used, but to do this you'll need a good equaliser. Parametric plug-ins designed for mastering or other high-quality applications produce the best results, and mastering engineers often manage to make music sound louder and clearer than it is by cutting the mid range slightly, adding a small amount of high-end boost at around 12kHz and possibly boosting the bass at around 80Hz, if the mix is lacking in punch. Be very sparing with the amount of EQ you add, however, and always patch the EQ after the compressor, or you'll find that the compressor tries to undo some of the work you're doing with the equaliser.

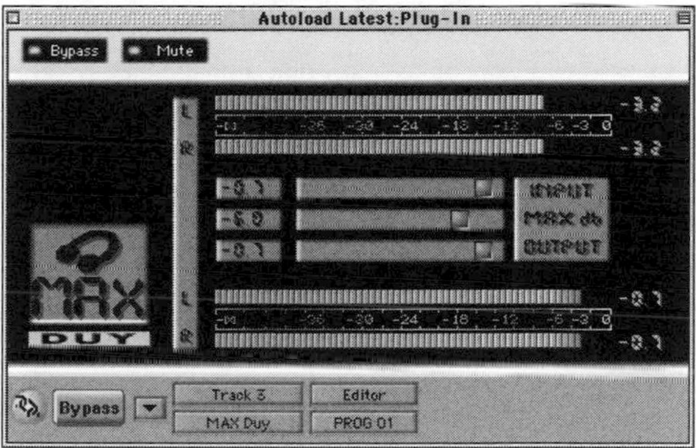

Figure 4.1: DUY's MAX limiter plug-in

enhancers

It may also be beneficial to treat an entire mix with an enhancer, especially if you feel that it's lacking clarity. Enhancement increases the listener's perceived sense of loudness and detail. Be careful not to apply too much, however, as your ears soon get used to the effect. I usually try to get the job done by using EQ first – a broadband boost of a decibel or two at between 12kHz and 15kHz can sometimes perform wonders in improving clarity and adding "air" to a mix – but if you feel that you need a little extra help, use just a touch of enhancement as well.

assessing your mix

Listen to your mix on as many different speaker systems as possible – including car systems and domestic hi-fis – before you pronounce it finished. Studio monitors can be very misleading, especially in untreated domestic rooms, so it's essential to test a mix at a moderate listening level on a pair of small speakers. Avoid the temptation of mixing at too high a volume, as this will only compromise your hearing judgement. The best guideline is to listen to your mix at the same level as that at which you'd expect the end user to be hearing it.

denoising

If you record and mix carefully, you shouldn't be unduly troubled by noise, but occasionally there are pieces of equipment that generate more hiss than they should, especially old analogue synths. Gates are of little use here, because in serious cases the hiss will still be audible over the audio when the gate is open. Fortunately, there are denoising plug-ins available that can bring about dramatic improvements, although these can introduce undesirable side-effects if used too much.

The best denoisers work by splitting the audio into a very large number of frequency bands and then processing each of them with an expander. Systems with in excess of 500 frequency bands are not uncommon, and because there are so many bands, their ability to remove noise is much improved – instead of muting the whole signal when the gate closes, they mute only the part of the spectrum where there is little or no activity.

Clearly, it wouldn't be practical to configure all of these bands manually, and so most systems work by "fingerprinting" a short section of noise from the start or the end of a song. The spectral content of the noise is then used to determine the expander thresholds automatically in order to perform the least obtrusive noise-reduction processing. A typical plug-in will include a control that lets you decide the amount by which you want to reduce the noise contribution, and intuitively you might feel that this should be set as high as possible. However, if you set this value to maximum, you'll probably hear a low-level chirping or tinkling sound as the various frequency bands switch on and off. Some plug-ins cope with this problem better than others, but the best strategy seems to be to adjust the noise-reduction control until the background noise just about masks the side-effects. In most cases, this will still reduce the background noise by a degree sufficient to make a serious improvement to the subjective sound quality.

Figure 4.2 shows TC Works' Spark denoising plug-in, which can be used within VST applications via the Spark FX Machine.

mixing overview

There isn't space in this book to go into the whole mixing process in detail, but I've put together this quick checklist that you may find useful to follow until you've gained enough experience to come up with a method that works well for you and your music.

Figure 4.2: TC Works' Spark denoising plug-in

- Start by setting up a basic mix without EQ or effects and clean up any unwanted pauses in your audio tracks.

- Listen closely to hear how the vocals sit with the backing track. Use a VST compressor plug-in to smoothe out the vocal levels and add some reverb with a suitable plug-in connected to the aux send. If your mix seems too busy, consider removing parts or selecting different sounds. You can also use high and low shelving filter plug-ins to trim away excessive high and low frequencies from any sound that's taking up too much space in a mix. For example, you can often trim away some low end from VST instrument synth pads or acoustic guitar recordings to make the part sit better in the mix. With electric guitars, you may be able to trim away both high and low end to tidy up the sound.

- Don't be afraid to automate your VST plug-ins if you feel that it would be useful for an effect to change character at different points within a song. Some obvious things to try are changing delay levels or reverb decay times, but you can also change the rate of modulation effects and automate filter sweeps. Dance music production invites experimentation, and many of the classic dance effects came about simply by users pushing the limits of their software to see what would happen.

- If you're still having difficulty, balance up the drum and bass sounds first and then add the vocals and other instruments. In most cases, the vocal track is the most important element of a song, so make sure that the rest of the track supports it and doesn't conflict with it instead.

- Use effects sparingly, unless the musical style in which you're working relies on sonic drama! Avoid using an excessively long reverb time on the vocals, unless the mix leaves space for such an effect. Listen to commercial recordings to hear how effects are used on these. In most cases, the application is quite subtle.

- Pan the instruments and effects to their desired positions, keeping bass sounds and lead vocals in the centre. If mono compatibility is important, as it is in a mix destined for TV or radio, switch back and forth between mono and stereo monitoring, listening out for any serious changes in level or strange tonal effects.

- You may find some benefit in adding a little

compression to a complete mix, although this shouldn't be considered compulsory. A compressor with an auto-attack/-release feature may cope best with the shifting dynamics of a real mix and a soft-knee expander will usually provide the most transparent results. Multiband compressors are the best to use for processing a mix, but in any event it's best to use low ratio settings and then set the threshold for around a maximum of 6dB of gain reduction.

- Subtle use of an enhancer and/or a good-quality equaliser plug-in can help separate individual sounds and emphasise detail.

common cable connections

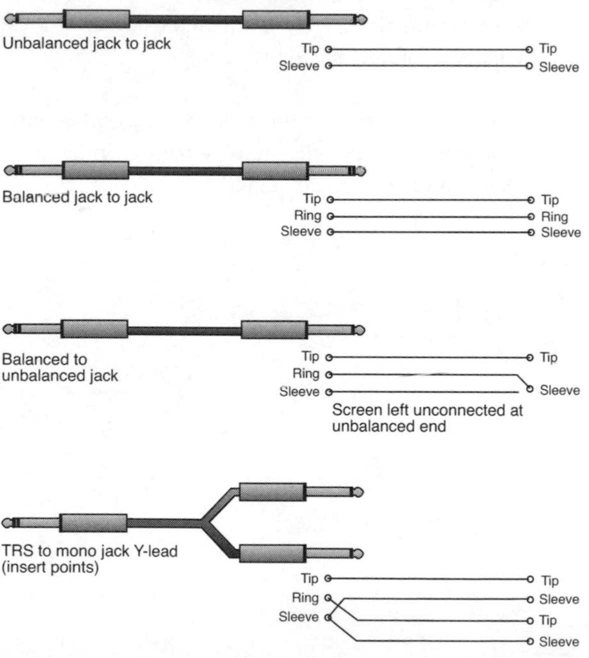

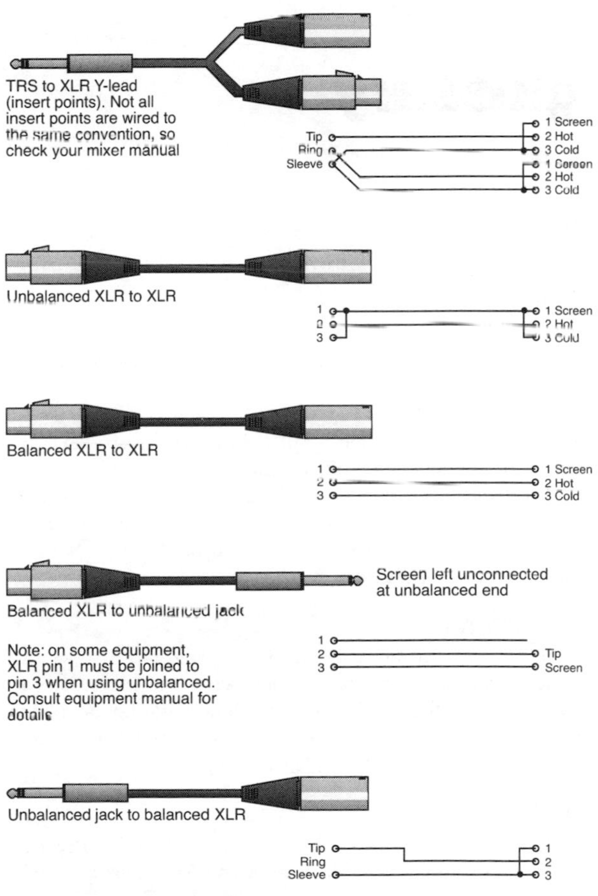
TRS to XLR Y-lead (insert points). Not all insert points are wired to the same convention, so check your mixer manual
Tip
Ring
Sleeve
1 Screen
2 Hot
3 Cold
1 Screen
2 Hot
3 Cold
Unbalanced XLR to XLR
1
2
3
1 Screen
2 Hot
3 Cold
Balanced XLR to XLR
1
2
3
1 Screen
2 Hot
3 Cold
Screen left unconnected at unbalanced end
Balanced XLR to unbalanced jack
Note: on some equipment, XLR pin 1 must be joined to pin 3 when using unbalanced. Consult equipment manual for details
1
2
3
Tip
Screen
Unbalanced jack to balanced XLR
Tip
Ring
Sleeve
1
2
3

glossary

AC

Abbreviation of Alternating Current.

active

Circuit containing transistors, ICs, tubes and other devices that require power to operate and are capable of amplification.

active sensing

System used to verify that a MIDI connection is working, in which the sending device frequently sends short messages to the receiving device to reassure it that all is well. If these active sensing messages stop for any reason, the receiving device will recognise a fault condition and switch off all notes. Not all MIDI devices support active sensing.

A/D converter

Circuit for converting analogue waveforms into a series of values represented by binary numbers. The more bits a converter has the greater the resolution of the sampling process. Current effects units are generally 16 bits or more, with the better models being either 20 or 24 bit.

ADSR

Envelope generator with Attack, Decay, Sustain and Release parameters. This is a simple type of envelope generator and was first used on early analogue synthesisers, though similar envelopes may be found in some effects units to control filter sweeps and suchlike.

aftertouch

Means of generating a control signal based on how much pressure is applied to the keys of a MIDI keyboard. Most instruments that support this do not have independent pressure sensing for all keys but instead detect the overall pressure by means of a sensing strip running beneath the keys. Aftertouch may be used to control musical functions such as vibrato depth, filter brightness, loudness and so on, though it may also be used to control some parameter of a MIDI effects unit, such as delay feedback or effect level.

algorithm

Computer program designed to perform a specific task. In the context of effects units, the term usually describes a software building block designed to create a specific effect or combination of effects. All digital effects are based on algorithms.

aliasing

When an analogue signal is sampled for conversion into a digital data stream, the sampling frequency must be at least twice that of the highest frequency component of the input signal. If this rule is disobeyed, the sampling process becomes ambiguous, as there are insufficient points to define each waveform cycle, resulting in enharmonic sum and difference frequencies being added to the audible signal.

ambience

Result of sound reflections in a confined space being added to the original sound. Ambience may also be created electronically by some digital reverb units. The main difference between ambience and reverberation is that ambience doesn't have the characteristic long delay time of reverberation – the reflections mainly give the sound a sense of space.

amp

Unit of electrical current, short for *ampère*.

amplifier

Device that increases the level of an electrical signal.

amplitude

Another word for level. Can refer to levels of sound or electrical signal.

analogue

Term used to describe circuitry that uses a continually-changing voltage or current to represent a signal. The origin of the term is that the electrical signal can be thought of as being analogous to the original signal.

anti-aliasing filter

Filter used to limit the frequency range of an analogue signal prior to A/D conversion so that the maximum frequency does not exceed half the sampling rate.

attack

Time that it takes for a sound to achieve its maximum amplitude. Drum sounds have a fast attack, whereas bowed string sounds have a slow attack. In compressors and gates, the attack time equates to how quickly the processor can change its gain.

attenuate

To make lower in level.

audio frequency

Signals in the human audio range, nominally 20Hz-20kHz.

aux

Control on a mixing console designed to route a proportion of the channel signal to the effects or cue mix outputs. (See "Aux Send".)

aux return

Mixer inputs used to add effects to the mix.

aux send

Physical output from a mixer aux send buss.

back-up

Safety copy of software or other digital data.

bandpass filter

Filter that removes or attenuates frequencies above and below the frequency at which it is set. Frequencies within the band are emphasised. Bandpass filters are often used in synthesisers as tone-shaping elements.

bandwidth

Means of specifying the range of frequencies passed by an electronic circuit such as an amplifier, mixer or filter. The frequency range is usually measured at the points where the level drops by 3dB relative to the maximum.

binary

Counting system based on only two numbers, one and zero.

boost/cut control

Single control that allows the range of frequencies passing through a filter to be either amplified or attenuated. The centre position is usually the "flat" or "no effect" position.

bouncing

Process of mixing two or more recorded tracks together and re-recording these onto another track.

BPM

Abbreviation of Beats Per Minute.

breath controller

Device that converts breath pressure into MIDI controller data.

buffer

Circuit designed to isolate the output of a source device from loading effects due to the input impedance of the destination device.

buffer memory

Temporary RAM memory used in some computer operations, sometimes to prevent a break in the data stream when the computer is interrupted to perform another task.

buss

Common electrical signal path along which signals may travel. In a mixer, there are several busses carrying the stereo mix, the groups, the PFL signal, the aux sends and so on. Power supplies are also fed along busses.

chase

Term describing the process whereby a slave device attempts to synchronise itself with a master device. In the context of a MIDI sequence, Chase may also involve chasing events (looking back to earlier positions in the song to see if there are any program changes or other events that need to be acted upon).

chorus

Effect created by doubling a signal and adding delay and pitch modulation.

chromatic

Describes a scale of pitches rising in steps of one semitone .

clipping

Severe form of distortion that occurs when a signal attempts to exceed the maximum level that a piece of equipment can handle.

compander

Encode/decode device that compresses a signal while encoding it and then expands it when decoding it.

compressor

Device designed to reduce the dynamic range of audio signals by reducing the level of high signals or by increasing the level of low signals.

console

Alternative term for mixer.

continuous controller

Type of MIDI message used to translate continuous change, such as from a pedal, wheel or breath control device.

copy protection

Method used by software manufacturers to prevent unauthorised copying.

crash

Slang term relating to malfunction of a computer program.

cut-and-paste editing

Copying or moving sections of a recording to different locations.

cut-off frequency

Frequency above or below which attenuation begins in a filter circuit.

daisy chain

Term used to describe serial electrical connection between devices or modules.

damping

In the context of reverberation, damping refers to the rate at which reverberant energy is absorbed by the various surfaces in an environment.

DAT

Abbreviation of Digital Audio Tape. The most commonly-used DAT machines are more correctly known as R-DATs because they use a rotating head similar to that in a video recorder. Digital recorders using fixed or stationary heads (such as DCC) are known as S-DAT machines.

data

Information stored and used by a computer.

data compression

System for reducing the amount of data stored by a digital system. Most audio data compression systems are known as lossy systems, because some of the original signal is discarded in accordance with psychoacoustic principles designed to ensure that only components that cannot be heard are lost.

dB

Abbreviation of Decibel, a unit used to express the relative levels of two electrical voltages, powers or sounds.

dB per octave

Means of measuring the slope of a filter. The more decibels per octave the sharper the filter slope.

DC

Abbreviation of Direct Current.

DCC

Stationary-head digital recorder format developed by Philips. Uses a data-compression system to reduce the amount of data that needs to be stored.

decay

Progressive reduction in amplitude of a sound or electrical signal over time. In the context of an ADSR envelope shaper, the decay phase starts as soon as the attack phase has reached its maximum level. In the decay phase, the signal level drops until it reaches the sustain level set by the user. The signal then remains at this level until the key is released, at which point the release phase is entered.

de-esser

Device for reducing the effect of sibilance in vocal signals.

defragmentation

Process of rearranging the files on a hard disk so that all of the files are as contiguous as possible, and that the remaining free space is also contiguous.

digital delay

Digital processor for generating delay and echo effects.

digital reverb

Digital processor for simulating reverberation.

DIN connector

Consumer multipin signal connection format, also used for MIDI cabling. Various pin configurations are available.

direct coupling

Means of connecting two electrical circuits so that both AC and DC signals may be passed between them.

disc

Term used to describe vinyl discs, CDs and MiniDiscs.

disk

Abbreviation of diskette now used to describe computer floppy, hard and removable disks. (See "Floppy Disk".)

DOS

Disk Operating System. Part of the operating system of PC and PC-compatible computers.

driver

Piece of software that handles communications between the main program and a hardware peripheral, such as a soundcard, printer or scanner.

drum pad

Synthetic playing surface that produces electronic trigger signals in response to being hit with drumsticks.

dry

Signal to which no effects have been added. Conversely, a sound that has been treated with an effect, such as reverberation, is referred to as wet.

DSP

Abbreviation of Digital Signal Processor. A powerful microchip used to process digital signals.

dubbing

Adding further material to an existing recording. Also known as overdubbing.

ducking

System for controlling the level of one audio signal with another. For example, background music can be made to duck whenever there is a voice-over.

dump

To transfer digital data from one device to another. A sysex dump is a means of transmitting information about a particular instrument or module over MIDI, and may be used to store sound patches, parameter settings and so on.

dynamic range

Range in decibels between the highest signal that can be handled by a piece of equipment and the level at which small signals disappear into the noise floor.

dynamics

Method of describing the relative levels within a piece of music.

early reflections

First sound reflections from walls, floors and ceilings following a sound that is created in an acoustically reflective environment.

effects loop

Connection system that allows an external signal processor to be connected into the audio chain.

effects return

Additional mixer input designed to accommodate the output from an effects unit.

effects unit

Device for treating an audio signal in order to change it in some creative way. Effects often involve the use of delay circuits, and include such treatments as reverb and echo.

enhancer

Device designed to brighten audio material using techniques such as dynamic equalisation, phase shifting and harmonic generation.

envelope
Graph charting the way in which the level of a sound or signal varies over time.

envelope generator
Circuit capable of generating a control signal that represents the envelope of the sound you want to recreate. This may then be used to control the level of an oscillator or other sound source, though envelopes may also be used to control filter or modulation settings. The most common example is the ADSR generator.

equaliser
Device that cuts or boosts selected parts of the audio spectrum.

exciter
Enhancer synthesises new high-frequency harmonics.

expander
Device designed to decrease the level of low-level signals and increase the level of high-level signals, thus increasing the dynamic range of the signal.

expander module
Synthesiser with no keyboard, often rack mountable or in some other compact format.

fader
Sliding potentiometer used in mixers and other processors.

filter
Electronic circuit designed to emphasise or attenuate a specific range of frequencies.

flanging
Modulated delay effect using feedback to create a dramatic, sweeping sound.

floppy disk
Computer disk that uses a flexible magnetic medium encased in a protective plastic sleeve. The maximum capacity of a standard high-density disk is 1.44MB. Earlier double-density disks hold only around half that amount of data.

formant
Frequency component or resonance of an instrument or voice sound that doesn't change with the pitch of the note being played or sung. For example, the body resonance of an acoustic guitar remains constant regardless of the note being played.

formatting
Procedure required to make a computer disk ready to be used. Formatting organises the disk's surface into a series of electronic pigeonholes into which data can then be stored. Different types of computer often use different formatting systems.

fragmentation
Process by which the available space on a disk drive is split up into small sections due to the storing and erasing of files. (See "Defragmentation".)

frequency
Indication of how many cycles of a repetitive waveform occur in one second. A waveform that has a repetition cycle of once per second has a frequency of 1Hz.

frequency response

Measurement of the frequency range that can be handled by a specific piece of electrical equipment or loudspeaker.

fundamental

Any sound comprises a fundamental or basic frequency plus harmonics and partials at a higher frequency.

FX

Abbreviation of effects.

gain

Amount by which a circuit amplifies a signal.

gate

Electrical signal that is generated whenever a key is depressed on an electronic keyboard. This is used to trigger envelope generators and other events that need to be synchronised to key action.

gate

Electronic device designed to mute low-level signals, thus improving the noise performance during pauses in the wanted material.

General MIDI

Addition to the basic MIDI specification to assure a minimum level of compatibility when playing back GM-format song files. The specification covers type and program, number of sounds, minimum levels of polyphony and multitimbrality, response to controller information and so on.

glitch

Describes an unwanted short-term corruption of a signal, or the unexplained short-term malfunction of a piece of equipment. For example, an inexplicable click on a DAT tape would be termed a glitch.

graphic equaliser

Equaliser on which several narrow segments of the audio spectrum are controlled by individual cut/boost faders. The name derives from the fact that the fader positions provide a graphic representation of the EQ curve.

group

Collection of signals within a mixer that are mixed and then routed through a separate fader to provide overall control. In a multitrack mixer, several groups are provided to feed the various recorder track inputs.

GS

Roland's own extension to the General MIDI protocol.

hard disk

High-capacity computer storage device based on a rotating rigid disk with a magnetic coating onto which data may be recorded.

harmonic

High-frequency component of a complex waveform.

harmonic distortion

Addition of harmonics not present in the original signal.

head

Part of a tape machine or disk drive that reads and/or writes data to and from the storage media.

headroom

Safety margin in decibels between the highest peak signal being passed by a piece of equipment and the absolute maximum level the equipment can handle.

high-pass filter

Filter that attenuates frequencies below its cut-off frequency.

hiss

Noise caused by random electrical fluctuations.

hum

Signal contamination caused by the addition of low frequencies, usually related to the mains power frequency.

Hz

Abbreviation of Hertz, the unit of frequency.

insert point

Connector that allows an external processor to be patched into a signal path so that the signal then flows through the external processor.

interface

Device that acts as an intermediary to two or more other pieces of equipment. For example, a MIDI interface enables a computer to communicate with MIDI instruments and keyboards.

intermodulation distortion

Form of distortion that introduces frequencies not present in the original signal. These are invariably based on the sum and difference products of the original frequencies.

IRQ

Abbreviation of Interrupt Request, part of the operating system of a computer that allows a connected device to request attention from a processor in order to transfer data to or from it.

jack

Common audio connector. May be mono (TS) or stereo (TRS).

k

Abbreviation of 1,000 (ie *kilo*). Used as a prefix to other values to indicate magnitude.

LCD

Abbreviation of Liquid Crystal Display.

LED

Abbreviation of Light-Emitting Diode, a solid-state lamp.

LFO

Oscillator used as a modulation source, usually below 20Hz. The most common LFO waveshape is the sine wave, although you can often choose sine, square, triangular or sawtooth waveforms.

LSB

Abbreviation of Least Significant Byte. If a piece of data has to be conveyed as two bytes, one byte represents high-value numbers and the other low-value numbers, in much the same way as tens and units function in the decimal system. The high value, or most significant part of the message, is called the Most Significant Byte or MSB.

limiter

Device that controls the gain of a signal so as to prevent it from ever exceeding a preset level. A limiter is essentially a fast-acting compressor with an infinite compression ratio.

linear

Device where the output is a direct multiple of the input.

line level

Mixers and signal processors tend to work at a standard signal level known as line level. In practice there are several different standard line levels, but all are in the order of a few volts. A nominal signal level is around -10dBv for semi-pro equipment and +4dBv for professional equipment.

load

Electrical circuit that draws power from another circuit or power supply. Also describes reading data into a computer.

loop

Circuit where the output is connected back to the input.

low-pass filter

A filter that attenuates frequencies above its cut-off frequency.

mA

Milliamp, or one thousandth of an amp.

MDM

Modular Digital Multitrack. A digital recorder that can be used in multiples to provide a greater number of synchronised tracks than a single machine.

memory

Computer's RAM memory used to store programs and data. This data is lost when the computer is switched off and so must be stored to disk or other suitable media.

menu

List of choices presented by a computer program or a device with a display window.

mic level

Low-level signal generated by a microphone. This must be amplified many times to increase it to line level.

microprocessor

Specialised microchip at the heart of a computer. It is here that instructions are read and acted upon.

MIDI

Abbreviation of Musical Instrument Digital Interface.

MIDI analyser

Device that gives a visual readout of MIDI activity when connected between two pieces of MIDI equipment.

MIDI bank change

Type of controller message used to select alternate banks of MIDI programs where access to more than 128 programs is required.

MIDI controller

Term used to describe the physical interface by means of which the musician plays the MIDI synthesiser or other sound generator. Examples of controllers are keyboards, drum pads, wind synths and so on.

MIDI control change

Also known as MIDI Controllers or Controller Data. These messages convey positional information relating to performance controls such as wheels, pedals, switches and other devices. This information can be used to control functions such as vibrato depth, brightness, portamento, effects levels, and many other parameters.

(standard) MIDI file

Standard file format for storing song data recorded on a MIDI sequencer in such as way as to allow it to be read by other makes or models of MIDI sequencer.

MIDI implementation chart

Chart found usually in MIDI product manuals that provides information as to which MIDI features are supported. Supported features are marked with a 0 while unsupported feature are marked with a X. Additional information may be provided, such as the exact form of the bank change message.

MIDI in

Socket used to receive information from a master controller or from the MIDI Thru socket of a slave unit.

MIDI merge

Device or sequencer function that enables two or more streams of MIDI data to be combined.

MIDI mode

MIDI information can be interpreted by the receiving MIDI instrument in a number of ways, the most common being polyphonically on a single MIDI channel (poly-omni off mode). Omni mode enables a MIDI Instrument to play all incoming data regardless of channel.

MIDI module

Sound-generating device with no integral keyboard.

MIDI note number

Every key on a MIDI keyboard has its own note number, ranging from 0 to 127, where 60 represents middle C. Some systems use C3 as middle C while others use C4.

MIDI note off

MIDI message sent when key is released.

MIDI note on

Message sent when note is pressed.

MIDI out

MIDI connector used to send data from a master device to the MIDI In of a connected slave device.

MIDI port

MIDI connections of a MIDI-compatible device. A multiport, in the context of a MIDI interface, is a device with multiple MIDI output sockets, each capable of carrying data relating to a different set of 16 MIDI channels. Multiports are the only means of exceeding the limitations imposed by 16 MIDI channels.

MIDI program change

Type of MIDI message used to change sound patches on a remote module or the effects patch on a MIDI effects unit.

MIDI splitter

Alternative term for MIDI thru box.

MIDI sync
Description of the synchronisation systems available to MIDI users: MIDI Clock and MIDI Time Code.

MIDI thru
Socket on a slave unit used to feed the MIDI In socket of the next unit in line.

MIDI thru box
Device that splits the MIDI Out signal of a master instrument or sequencer to avoid daisy chaining. Powered circuitry is used to "buffer" the outputs so as to prevent problems when many pieces of equipment are driven from a single MIDI output.

mixer
Device for combining two or more audio signals.

monitor
Reference loudspeaker used for mixing.

monitor
VDU for a computer.

monitoring
Action of listening to a mix or a specific audio signal.

monophonic
Term used to describe the playing of one note at a time.

multisample
Creation of several samples, each covering a limited musical range, the idea being to produce a more natural range of sounds across the range of the instrument being sampled. For

example, a piano may need to be sampled every two or three semitones in order to sound convincing.

multitimbral module

MIDI sound source capable of producing several different sounds at the same time and controlled on different MIDI channels.

multitrack

Recording device capable of recording several "parallel" parts or tracks that may then be mixed or re-recorded independently.

noise reduction

System for reducing analogue tape noise or for reducing the level of hiss present in a recording.

noise shaping

System for creating digital dither so that any added noise is shifted into those parts of the audio spectrum where the human ear is least sensitive.

octave

When a frequency or pitch is transposed up by one octave, its frequency is doubled.

offline

Process carried out while a recording is not playing. For example, some computer-based processes have to be carried out offline as the computer isn't fast enough to carry out the process in real time.

operating system

Basic software that enables a computer to load and run other programs.

oscillator
Circuit designed to generate a periodic electrical waveform.

overdub
To add another part to a multitrack recording or to replace one of the existing parts. (See "Dubbing").

overload
To exceed the operating capacity of a circuit.

pad
Resistive circuit for reducing signal level.

parallel
Method of connecting two or more circuits together so that their inputs and outputs are all connected together.

parameter
Variable value that affects some aspect of a device's performance.

parametric EQ
Equaliser with separate controls for frequency, bandwidth and cut/boost.

passive
Circuit with no active elements.

patch
Alternative term for program. Referring to a single programmed

sound within a synthesiser that can be called up using program-change commands. MIDI effects units and samplers also have patches.

patch bay

System of panel-mounted connectors used to bring inputs and outputs to a central point from where they can be routed using plug-in patch cords.

patch cord

Short cable used with patch bays.

peak

Maximum instantaneous level of a signal.

peak

The highest signal level in any section of programme material.

PFL

Abbreviation of Pre-Fade Listen, a system used within a mixing console to allow the operator to listen in on a selected signal, regardless of the position of the fader controlling that signal.

phase

Timing difference between two electrical waveforms expressed in degrees where 360° corresponds to a delay of exactly one cycle.

phaser

Effect that combines a signal with a phase-shifted version of itself to produce creative filtering effects. Most phasers are controlled by means of an LFO.

phono plug
Hi-fi connector developed by RCA and used extensively on semi-pro, unbalanced recording equipment.

pick-up
Part of a guitar that converts string vibrations to electrical signals.

pitch
Musical interpretation of an audio frequency.

pitch bend
Special control message specifically designed to produce a change in pitch in response to the movement of a pitch bend wheel or lever. Pitch bend data can be recorded and edited, just like any other MIDI controller data, even though it isn't part of the controller message group.

pitch shifter
Device for changing the pitch of an audio signal without changing its duration.

polyphony
Term used to describe an instrument's ability to play two or more notes simultaneously. An instrument that can play only one note at a time is described as monophonic.

port
Connection for the input or output of data.

portamento
Gliding effect that allows a sound to change pitch gradually instead of abruptly when a new key is pressed or MIDI note sent.

post-production

Work done to a stereo recording after mixing is complete.

post-fade

Aux signal taken from after the channel fader so that the aux send level follows any channel fader changes. Normally used for feeding effects devices.

pre-fade

Aux signal taken from before the channel fader so that the channel fader has no effect on the aux send level. Normally used for creating foldback or cue mixes.

preset

Effects unit or synth patch that cannot be altered by the user.

pressure

Alternative term for aftertouch.

processor

Device designed to treat an audio signal by changing its dynamics or frequency content. Examples of processors include compressors, gates and equalisers.

program change

MIDI message designed to change instrument or effects unit patches.

pulse wave

Similar to a square wave but non-symmetrical. Pulse waves sound brighter and thinner than square waves, making them useful in the synthesis of reed instruments. The timbre changes according to the mark/space ratio of the waveform.

pulse-width modulation

Means of modulating the duty cycle (mark/space ratio) of a pulse wave. This changes the timbre of the basic tone. LFO modulation of pulse width can be used to produce a pseudo-chorus effect.

punch-in

Action of placing an already recorded track into record at the correct time during playback so that the existing material may be extended or replaced.

punch-out

Action of switching a tape machine (or other recording device) out of record after executing a punch in. With most multitrack machines, both punching in and punching out can be accomplished without stopping the tape.

Q

Measurement of the resonant properties of a filter. The higher the Q, the more resonant the filter and the narrower the range of frequencies that are allowed to pass.

quantising

Means of moving notes recorded in a MIDI sequencer so that they line up with user defined subdivisions of a musical bar – 16s, for example. The facility may be used to correct timing errors, but over-quantising can remove the human feel from a performance.

RAM

Abbreviation for Random Access Memory. This is a type of memory used by computers for the temporary storage of programs and data, and all data is lost when the power is turned off. For that reason, work needs to be saved to disk if it is not to be lost.

R-DAT

Digital tape machine that uses a rotating head system.

real time

An audio process that can be carried out as the signal is being recorded or played back takes place in real time. The opposite is offline, where the signal is processed in non-real time.

release

Time taken for a level or gain to return to normal. Often used to describe the rate at which a synthesised sound reduces in level after a key has been released.

resistance

Opposition to the flow of electrical current. Measured in ohms.

resolution

Accuracy with which an analogue signal is represented by a digitising system. The more bits are used, the more accurately the amplitude of each sample can be measured, but there are other elements of converter design that also affect accuracy. High conversion accuracy is known as high resolution.

resonance

Same as Q.

reverb

Acoustic ambience created by multiple reflections in a confined space.

RF
Radio Frequency.

RF interference
Interference significantly above the range of human hearing.

ribbon microphone
Microphone in which the sound-capturing element is a thin metal ribbon suspended in a magnetic filed. When sound causes the ribbon to vibrate, a small electrical current is generated within the ribbon.

RMS
Abbreviation of Root Mean Square, a method of specifying the behaviour of a piece of electrical equipment under continuous sine wave testing conditions.

roll-off
The rate at which a filter attenuates a signal once it has passed the filter cut-off point.

ROM
Abbreviation of Read-Only Memory. This is a permanent and non-volatile type of memory containing data that can't be changed. Operating systems are often stored on ROM as the memory remains intact when the power is switched off.

sample
Process carried out by an A/D converter where the instantaneous amplitude of a signal is measured many times per second (44.1kHz in the case of CD).

sample

Digitised sound used as a musical sound source in a sampler or additive synthesiser.

sample and hold

Usually refers to a feature whereby random values are generated at regular intervals and then used to control another function such as pitch or filter frequency. Sample and hold circuits were also used in old analogue synthesisers to "remember" the note being played after a key had been released.

sample rate

Number of times that an A/D converter samples the incoming waveform each second.

sawtooth wave

So called because it resembles the teeth of a saw, this waveform contains only even harmonics.

SCSI

Abbreviation of Small Computer System Interface, pronounced "skuzzi". An interfacing system for using hard drives, scanners, CD-ROM drives and similar peripherals with a computer. Each SCSI device has its own ID number and no two SCSI devices in the same chain must be set to the same number. The last SCSI device in the chain should be terminated either via an internal terminator, where provided, or via a plug-in terminator fitted to a free SCSI socket.

sequencer

Device for recording and replaying MIDI data, usually in a multitrack format, allowing complex compositions to be built up a part at a time.

sibilance

High-frequency whistling or lisping sound that affects vocal recordings due either to poor mic technique or excessive equalisation.

signal

Electrical representation of input such as sound.

signal chain

Route taken by a signal from the input of a system to its output.

signal-to-noise ratio

Ratio of maximum signal level to the residual noise, expressed in decibels.

sine wave

Waveform of a pure tone with no harmonics.

slave

Device under the control of a master device.

SMPTE

Time code developed for the film industry but now extensively used in music and recording. SMPTE is a real-time code and is related to hours, minutes, seconds and film or video frames rather than to musical tempo.

step time

System for programming a sequencer in non-real time.

stereo

Two-channel system feeding left and right loudspeakers.

square wave

Symmetrical rectangular waveform. Square waves contain a series of odd harmonics.

sub-bass

Frequencies below the range of typical monitor loudspeakers. Some define sub-bass as frequencies that can be felt rather than heard.

subcode

Hidden data within the CD and DAT format that includes such information as the absolute time location, number of tracks, total running time and so on.

subtractive synthesis

Process of creating a new sound by filtering and shaping a raw, harmonically complex waveform. Can be thought of as similar to whittling a piece of wood.

sustain

Part of the ADSR envelope that determines the level to which the sound will settle if a key is held down. Once the key is released, the sound decays at a rate set by the release parameter. Also refers to a guitar's ability to hold notes that decay very slowly.

synthesiser

Electronic musical instrument designed to create a wide range of sounds, both imitative and abstract.

tempo

Rate of the beat of a piece of music, measured here in beats per minute.

test tone

Steady, fixed-level tone recorded onto a multitrack or stereo recording to act as a reference when matching levels.

timbre

Tonal "colour" of a sound.

track

Term that dates back to multitrack tape, on which the tracks are physical stripes of recorded material located side by side along the length of the tape.

tracking

System whereby one device follows another. Tracking is often discussed in the context of MIDI guitar synthesisers or controllers where the MIDI output attempts to track the pitch of the guitar strings.

transducer

Device for converting one form of energy into another. A microphone is a good example of a transducer, as it converts mechanical energy to electrical energy.

transparency

Subjective term used to describe audio quality where the high-frequency detail is clear and individual sounds are easy to identify and separate.

transpose

To shift a musical signal by a fixed number of semitones.

tremolo

Modulation of the amplitude of a sound using an LFO.

triangle wave

Symmetrical, triangle-shaped wave containing only odd harmonics, but with a lower harmonic content than the square wave.

TRS jack

Stereo-type jack with tip, ring and sleeve connections.

unison

To play the same melody using two or more different instruments or voices.

valve

Vacuum-tube amplification component, also known as a tube.

velocity

Rate at which a key is depressed. This may be used to control loudness (to simulate the response of instruments such as pianos) or other parameters on later synthesisers.

vibrato

Pitch modulation using an LFO to modulate a VCO.

vocoder

Signal processor that imposes a changing spectral filter on a sound based on the frequency characteristics of a second sound. By taking the spectral content of a voice and imposing it on a musical instrument, talking-instrument effects can be created.

voice

Capacity of a synthesiser to play a single musical note. An instrument capable of playing 16 simultaneous notes is said to be a 16-voice instrument.

volt
Unit of electrical power.

VU meter
Meter designed to interpret signal levels in roughly the same way as the human ear, which responds more closely to the average levels of sounds rather than to the peak levels.

wah pedal
Guitar effects device where a bandpass filter is varied in frequency by means of a pedal control.

watt
Unit of electrical power.

waveform
Graphic representation of the way in which a sound wave or electrical wave varies with time.